Library of
Davidson College

Ivan Trufanov

PROBLEMS OF SOVIET URBAN LIFE

Leningrad, 1973

Translated, with notes, new introduction
and special bibliography by

James Riordan
University of Bradford
England

Oriental Research Partners
Newtonville, Mass.
1977

© Oriental Research Partners, 1977

Publisher's Note

This work is an unabridged translation of the Soviet work *Problemy byta gorodskogo naseleniya SSSR* by Ivan Trufanov of the Ministry of Higher and Secondary Specialised Education in the RSFSR. It was published by Leningrad University in 1973 with a press run of 3475 copies and a price of 70 kopecks.* The book reflects many of the Soviet views towards urban development with emphasis on the successful rather than the more troublesome aspects. The reader is invited to take this unique opportunity to examine this important example of current Soviet sociological study.

*As of July, 1977, one rouble is $1.30

ISBN 0-89250-008-5

For a detailed brochure on our Russian Series write to the Editor, Oriental Research Partners, Box 148, Newtonville, Mass. 02160.

Table of Contents

A Note on Translation i
Introductory Note . . . . ii-ix
Problems of Soviet Urban Life 1
Footnotes 105
Special Section (Bibliography compiled by Dr. James Riordan) . 118-125

A Note on Translation

As the author himself says, sociologists do not always speak the same language in a conceptual as well as a linguistic sense. Problems therefore arise both in conveying the Russian style (which tends to favour indirect, passive and circumlocutory forms) and in translating concepts and institutions for which no ready English equivalents exist. How does one translate, for example, the central theme of the book — *byt*, or the Soviet occupational grades — given the differences in classification of occupations and the absence of agreed definitions of them in the West? As a rule, I have used the nearest English equivalent, although sometimes I have had to invent a term. I give a list of the most common below. I have taken the liberty of making amendments to the text to imporve readability, while maintaining the sense and accuracy of the original. I have checked quotations of foreign authors with the original wherever possible, written (and sometimes corrected) foreign names in full where Western usage makes this desirable. Similarly, I have tidied up footnotes and tables according to Western practice (adding, for example, dates to which surveys refer). Transliteration of Russian technical terms has been kept as consistent as possible throughout.

Glossary of common non-equivalent terms

byt: everyday life, urban life
bytovoye obsluzhivanie: consumer services
dacha: country cottage
denezhny dokhod: cash earnings (after tax and benefits)
domashny inventar': household inventory, furniture and home equipment
dosug: leisure
dolzhnost': job-responsibility
ITR (inzhenerno-teckhnicheskie rabotniki): engineering and technical personnel (with a secondary technical or higher education)
Komsomol: Young Communist League
NOT (Nauchnaya Organizatsiya Truda): Scientific Organisation of Labour
obshchestvennaya rabota: social work
obshchestvennye fondy: public consumption funds
podsobnoye khozyaistvo: home farm
rabochiy: industrial manual worker
sadovo-ogorodny uchastok: garden allotment and orchard
sadovoi uchastok: garden allotment
samoobsluzhivanie: everyday domestic needs (shopping, cooking, laundry, etc.)
sluzhashchiy: employee
zakonomernost': pattern, law

INTRODUCTORY NOTE

Soviet urban sociology is essentially a product of the last decade. Only seven works were published on urbanisation problems in 1966, but as many as 50 in 1970[1]. The mounting interest is reflected in the wide range of studies: 40 of the bibliographical items deal with non-Soviet societies — from Japan and Afghanistan to Rhodesia and Argentina. Like the parent discipline sociology, Soviet urban studies have not become legitimate without a struggle and are still circumscribed by taboos and limitations. Nevertheless, Soviet urban researchers are gaining a professional standing at home as high as that attained in other disciplines and increasingly merit the attention abroad of students of sociology and of Soviet society.

The need for serious urban research is self-evident from a glance at changes in the rural-urban demographic balance (see Table 1).

Table 1

Growth in Urban Settlements and Size of Urban Population in the USSR, 1926-1970

Census years	Number		Total number of urban settlements	Size of Urban population (mln.)	Urban share of total population (%)
	Towns	Workers' settlements			
1926	709	1,216	1,925	26.3	18
1939	923	1,450	2,373	56.1	33
1959	1,679	2,940	4,619*	100.0	48
1970	1,935	3,569	5,499	136.0	56

Sources: *Itogi Vsesoyuznoi perepisi naseleniya 1959 goda. SSSR*, Moscow, Gosstatizdat, 1962, p.35; *O predvaritel'nykh itogakh Vsesoyuznoi perepisi naseleniya 1970 goda*, Moscow, Statistika, 1970, p.15.

As Table 1 shows, the urban share of the population rose from 18 per cent in 1917 to 56 per cent in 1970; between 1939 and 1970 alone, the urban share increased from 33 per cent to 56 per cent and the number of townsmen more than doubled. By the end of the century, it is estimated that three-quarters of the Soviet population will be urban[2]. Even so, the USSR is less urban than most urban-industrial Western states: in 1970, the urban percentages were 84 for the Netherlands, 79 for Sweden, 77 United Kingdom, 72 USA, 70 France and 66 Belgium[3].

While urbanisation in the USSR has been rapid, the rate has varied over time and place. The fastest urban growth rate occurred between 1926 and 1939, when the urban population rose by nearly 30 million, while the rural population fell by 6.2 million. "It has been estimated that a shift of labour comparable to that which took place in the USSR in the twelve years between 1928 and 1940, took from 30 to 50 years in the countries of Western Europe and the English speaking world that industrialised earlier."[4] But the urban growth has not been even. Today, three of the fifteen constituent republics (Russia, Latvia and Estonia) are over 60 per cent urban, and four are less than 40 per cent — Tadzhikistan and Kirgizia (both 37 per cent), Uzbekistan (36 per cent) and Moldavia (32 per cent). In the latter four, the percentage of urban dwellers among the indigenous native population is even lower and is likely to cause considerable labour difficulties in the next twenty years as the non-Russian ethnic group population in Central Asia and the Transcaucasus dynamically increases in comparison to the slow rate of growth in European Russia.[5]

The nature of this urban revolution and its concomittant problems differs in many ways from that of the West where urbanisation was less abrupt, caused less acute social upheaval and was played out largely with different personalities. The millions of peasants who poured into Soviet towns during the all-out industrialisation campaign of the 1930's had been serfs, literally slaves, not long before.[6] Their homes were not the terraced houses of the British industrial workers, but wooden shacks or barracks and, latterly, fairly cramped flats and hostels. The urbanisation process did not develop gradually as in the USA or Britain, but in leaps and bounds, involving acute changes of environment, ties, relations and a sharp break with the past. So great has been this human torrent that *all* major Soviet cities are now 'closed' to newcomers save those who can obtain a housing permit *(propusk)*. Even so, the population of Moscow has grown from 1,854,000 in 1917 to 7,500,000 in 1974[7] and there are now ten cities with a population of over a million, as against two in 1917. Table 2 gives some idea of the urban spread which should be used in conjunction with Table 3 — an employment table.

Table 2

Distribution of Soviet Urban Settlements by Size, 1926, 1959, 1973

All types of urban settlement (population)	Number of urban settlements			Number of residents in them (millions)		
	1926	1959	1973	1926	1959	1973
less than 3,000	748	843	1,108	1.2	1.6	2.0
3,000-5,000	320	904	1,036	1.3	3.6	4.1
5,000-10,000	378	1,296	1,480	2.7	9.2	10.5
10,000-20,000	253	798	966	3.5	11.2	13.5
20,000-50,000	135	474	611	4.0	14.8	18.8
50,000-100,000	60	156	207	4.1	11.0	14.2
100,000-500,000	28	123	201	5.4	24.4	42.2
500,000 and over	3	25	35	4.1	24.2	40.8
1,000,000 and over	2	3	10*	3.8	10.5	21.9*
Total	1,925	4,619	5,644	26.3	100.0	146.1

* figures for 1972

Sources: *Narodnoye khozyaistvo SSSR. 1922-1972 gg.*, Moscow, Statistika, 1972, p.19; *Narodnoye khozyaistvo SSSR v 1972 g.*, Moscow, Statistika, 1973, p.32

It is evident from the table that by early 1973, well over half the urban population of the USSR lived in relatively big towns of 100,000 or more, while between a quarter and a third lived in large cities of over half a million people.

Discussion of these figures and the data in Trufanov's book presupposes an understanding of the Soviet concept 'town'. Administrative definitions are based primarily on size of settlement and occupation of its inhabitants. Thus, P.I. Dubrovin writes: "A town is a diffuse social formation, being a place of mass settlement and a concentration of all forms of socially-useful activity except that involving hunting or primary agricultural production as the exclusive occupation of the population; it is organised in a constantly functioning economic-construction complex serving the everyday needs and activity of the population associated with it in accordance with the level of development of the forces of production."[8] This expressly utilitarian definition puts the accent

Table 3

Annual Average Employment in the National Economy, USSR:
1950 to 1974 (In thousands)

Line no.	Item	1950	1960	1964	1969	1970	1971	1972	1973	1974
1	Total	80,646	95,398	103,465	116,600	118,565	120,574	122,443	124,553	126,649
2	Nonagricultural sectors	37,611	55,404	65,191	78,861	81,012	83,306	85,601	87,537	89,684
3	Industry	15,317	22,620	26,317	31,159	31,593	32,030	32,461	32,875	33,433
4	Other nonagricultural sectors	21,666	32,619	38,773	47,680	49,413	51,270	53,134	54,706	56,245
5	Services[1]	13,091	18,447	22,829	28,649	29,615	30,670	31,763	32,870	33,849
6	Other[2]	8,575	14,172	15,944	19,031	19,793	20,600	21,371	21,836	22,396
7	Independent artisans	628	165	101	22	6	6	6	6	6
8	Agricultural sectors	43,035	39,994	38,274	37,739	37,553	37,268	36,842	36,966	36,965
9	State	3,437	6,793	8,168	9,083	9,180	9,499	9,647	9,885	10,102
10	Collective farm	27,600	22,300	19,200	17,500	17,000	16,500	16,200	16,100	15,900
11	Private	11,998	10,901	10,906	11,156	11,373	11,269	10,995	10,981	10,963
12	Socialised sector	68,020	84,332	92,458	105,422	107,186	109,299	111,442	113,566	115,680
13	Workers and employees	40,420	62,032	73,258	87,922	90,186	92,799	95,242	97,466	99,780
14	Collective farm	27,600	22,300	19,200	17,500	17,000	16,500	16,200	16,100	15,900
15	Private sector	12,626	11,066	11,007	11,178	11,379	11,375	11,001	10,987	10,969
16	Independent artisans	628	165	101	22	6	6	6	6	6
17	Private agriculture	11,998	10,901	10,905	11,156	11,373	11,269	10,995	10,981	10,963

[1] Includes trade, public dining, material-technical supply and sales, and procurement; housing-communal economy and personal services; education and culture; art; science and scientific services; credit and insurance organizations; and government administration.
[2] Includes construction; forestry; transport; communications; and other.

on density of population, *socially-useful* non-agricultural occupations and administrative organisation. But the town is one of two components of urban settlement; the other is the so-called urban-type workers' settlement. Opinions have varied over the boundaries between town and urban-type workers' settlement. For the 1970 Census, state statistical agencies classified as urban settlements the towns and urban-type workers' settlements with over 3,000 inhabitants, provided at least 75 per cent of the able-bodied population was engaged in non-agricultural pursuits.[9] Differences between the two depend on a number of factors, not necessarily size alone, but urban-type workers' settlements do not normally exceed 20,000 inhabitants.

The range of problems studied by Soviet urban sociologists has depended not simply on the idiosyncrasies of the urbanisation process; it has depended, too, on the exigencies of political planners concerned with the deliberate shaping of a new person and society according to communist principles. The political leaders see sociology generally "as an instrument which, by providing both information and analysis, helps to prevent the regime from losing contact with reality and which may help in planning and controlling society, as well as understanding it."[10] Urban sociologists, therefore, make their contribution by helping to reveal and solve particular 'concrete' problems; their approach is consequently empiricist and utilitarian, less concerned with the dynamics of the total society. As Trufanov explains (see pp. 34-35), Soviet social scientists do not regard sociology as ever being value-free. Inasmuch as a sociologist lives in a particular community, he reflects and expresses the values and attitudes of that society. Therefore, sociology is inevitably "a partisan science. The outlook of the social scientist, his social and political sympathies and his social position affect the methodology and even the methods of his research and, consequently, the results."[11] Within this conceptual framework, the Soviet researcher into urban problems studies deficiencies in society that prevent fulfilment of social goals, so that these obstacles may be removed. Since the prerequisites of complete communist society include the gradual effacement of the basic dividing lines between mental and manual workers, villagers and townsmen, men and women, and members of different ethnic groups, it is important to the political leaders to know how much has been achieved and what still needs to be done. Thus, this book directs attention to occupational, sex and ethnic differences and their reflection in the ways people live, what they read, how often they go to the cinema and theatre, what furniture and household equipment they possess, who bears the brunt of housework and child-care, etc. Another prerequisite of communism is a harmoniously-developed, cultured citizen; hence the concern here with the study of time-budgets to elicit whether leisure activity is being used 'rationally' for spiritual and physical development.

The immense value of Trufanov's work is that it is the first sociological study since the early 1920's to provide such a revealing insight into *actual* life and labour in a major Soviet city (Leningrad). Trufanov's findings are frank and often surprising; they are of undoubted interest to Western sociologists and students of Soviet society.

Many urban problems are, of course, common to all urbanising communities. Both Soviet and Western studies consider such factors as the changing distribution of skills, changes in the arrangements of occupations and the consequences for social ranking, the analysis of family patterns, ecological issues, the changing composition of the population, its distribution and how far it is given to being segregated or isolated with consequences for ethnic status, and so on. But fundamental differences do exist in the aims, approaches and methods of Soviet and Western urban sociologists which cannot be ignored. The Western urbanisation process is reflected in the parochial outlook of much of Western urban sociology, based as it is mainly on American cities. The Chicago school, after all, was conditioned by such problems as "unemployment, internal migration, immigration and ethnic group adjustment, crime and especially gang warfare."[12] It may be, in fact, that some Soviet experience in urban development may have more validity for urbanising states, particularly in the Third World, than that of the USA, Britain, France or Germany. Certainly, it merits attention both for comparative purposes and as an insight into Soviet society. What it does do most forcibly is to put to doubt the general applicability of much of Western urban sociology to the Soviet context. One obvious area of confusion is that of social stratification. Simply determining who falls into the category of a class clearly poses problems for a non-Marxist Western sociologist applying subjective criteria of class and other Western sociological concepts to Soviet society, yet at the same time utilising statistics compiled by Soviet social scientists. It is not strictly true, for example, that income acts as such a paramount yardstick for measuring positions in the Soviet stratification-hierarchy as it does in the West, because there would appear on the surface to be less coincidence of political, economic and social status in the Soviet Union, due to the fact that there are fewer things the average citizen can buy. (This does not take into account the small Party elite at the top of Soviet society who travel abroad, and buy Western goods at special currency shops in Russian cities — shops that are closed to the average Russian citizens.) Yet, it is not uncommon to find Western scholars applying solely that yardstick to Soviet society. Thus: "It has long been commonplace among Western sociologists to regard a person's income as an important — sometimes the most important — factor in determining his place in society. This is a sufficient reason for beginning our survey of the structure of the Soviet working class from that angle."[13] Since Trufanov, in common with other Soviet sociologists, uses a different approach to social stratification, it will be as well here to explain it briefly.

In Soviet conceptualising, class is determined by people's relationship to the means of production or, as Lenin put it, "by the place they occupy in a historically-defined system of social production, by their relationship ... to the means of production, by their role in the social organisation of labour and, consequently, by the size and method of acquiring the share of social wealth that they obtain."[14] Today, Soviet society is said by Soviet writers to consist of two non-antagonistic classes; the working class and the collective farmers. In most literature, the working class is, in fact, a shorthand term for all citizens who are not members of collective farms and is subdivided into the following two categories:

(i) *rabochie* = industrial manual workers – unskilled, semi-skilled and skilled. "Workers normally include people directly employed in manufacturing products or fulfilling auxiliary functions for manufacturing."[15] Since few jobs these days are utterly devoid of mental work, the criterion used to define a manual worker in the last two censuses has been that he should be employed *primarily* in physical work.[16]

(ii) *sluzhashchie* = employees, ranging from low-grade non-manual workers to highly-skilled engineering and technical personnel, from ice-cream sellers and shopgirls to writers and doctors. The main criterion is that they should be engaged *primarily* on mental work. "Employees include all persons engaged in administrative, managerial, accounting, supervisory and other functions which do not directly create any material values."[17]

This categorisation, though extremely broad, provides us with a rough guide to Trufanov's conceptual structure in regard to the urban population. Further explanatory notes are given as footnotes throughout the text.

James Riordan, University of Bradford 1977

Notes

1 Yu. L. Pivovarov (ed.), *Problemy sovremyennoi urbanizatsii*, Moscow, 1972, p.222.
2 *Ibid*., p.18. A good brief study with reference to other works on this aspect is W.A. Douglas Jackson, "Urban Expansion", *Problems of Communism*, XXIII, Nov - Dec., 1974, 14 - 24.
3 *United Nations Demographic Year Book*, Table 3.
4 C.E. Black, "Soviet Society: A Comparative View", in A. Kassof (ed.), *Prospects for Soviet Society*, Pall Mall Press, London, p.32.
5 Pivovarov, *op. cit.*, p. 144. For a very recent study on this acute problem of divergent demographic growths in the USSR, see Murray Feshback, Stephen Rapawy, "Population and Manpower Trends and Policies", a paper in U.S. Congress, Joint Economic Committee *Soviet Economy in a New Prespective*, 1976 (Washington, 1976).
6 Serfdom was abolished in 1861 although many remained tied to the land because of lack of money. The writer Victor Serge makes the instructive comparison that: "The abolition of serfdom in Russia coincides with the War of Secession and the abolition of slavery in the United States of America (1861-63). Both in the Old World and the New, the growth of capitalism demands the replacement of the slave or serf by the free worker – free, that is, to sell his toil. The free worker works better, more intensively and more conscientiously. Large mechanised industry is incompatible with primitive methods of compulsion; in their place it substitutes economic constraint,

the concealed compulsion of hunger whose efficacy is different in nature from that of naked violence" (see V. Serge, *Year One of the Russian Revolution*, Allen Lane, The Penguin Press, London, 1972, pp. 24-25.

7 *Narodnoye khozyaistvo SSSR. 1922-1972 gg.*, Moscow, 1972, p.19; "Krupneishy gorod Yevropy," *Sputnik*, No. 9, 1974, p. 49.

8 P.I. Dubrovin, "Aglomeratsiy gorodov (genesis, eknomika, morfologiya)," *Voprosy geografii*, sbornik 45. Geografiya gorodskikh i sel'skikh poseleniy, Moscow, 1959, p. 23.

9 M.L. Strongina, *Sotsial'no-ekonomicheskie problemy razvitiya bol'shikh gorodov v SSSR*, Moscow, 1970, p. 33. See also V.G. Davidovich, "O razvitii seti gorodov SSSR za 40 let," *Voprosy geografii*, sbornik 45. Geografiya gorodskikh i sel'skikh poseleniy, Moscow, 1959, p. 45.

10 E.A. Weinberg, *The Development of Sociology in the Soviet Union*, Routledge and Kegan Paul, London, 1974, p. 109.

11 V. Shlyapentokh, *Sotsiologiya dlya vsekh*, Moscow, 1970, p. 43.

12 G. Duncan Mitchell, *A Hundred Years of Sociology*, Duckworth, London, 1969, p. 275.

13 M. Matthews, *Class and Society in Soviet Russia*, Allen Lane, The Penguin Press, London, 1972, p. 72.

14 V.I. Lenin, *Collected Works* (Russian), Vol. 39, p. 15.

15 B.Ts. Urlanis, *Statistika naseleniya*, Moscow, 1971, p. 64. This division into two groups does, unfortunately, ignore the intelligentsia.

16 *Ibid.*, p. 65.

17 *Ibid.*, p. 64.

Some additional works to consult

Zev Katz, *Soviet Sociologists' Debate on Social Structure in the USSR; Soviet Dissenters and Social Structure in the USSR.* Both Cambridge, Mass, 1971. See Katz's other works, *Patterns of Social Stratification in the USSR;* (1972) *Patterns of Social Mobility in the USSR* (1973); *The Nachalnik-Executive-Class in the USSR* (1973) and two significant articles W.S. Smith, "Housing in the Soviet Union – Big Plans, Little Action", and F.A. Leedy, "Demographic Trends in the USSR", in Joint Economic Committee, 93rd U.S. Congress (ed.). *Soviet Economic Prospects for the Seventies: A Compendium of Papers* (Washington, 1973). A recent book by Hedrick Smith, *The Russians* (New York, 1976) is also useful for an interpretation of Soviet urban life based on four years of residence in the Soviet Union as the New York Times correspondent.

Ivan Trufanov

PROBLEMS OF SOVIET URBAN LIFE

Introduction

The Soviet Union is one of the world's highly urbanised countries: as many as 134,200,000 people, or 56 per cent of the Soviet population, lived in towns in 1969.[1] The increasing number of towns and townsmen is attributable to the high rate of economic progress. Understandably, rapid urban growth and the complex urban way of life are focusing attention on urbanisation and its attendant problems. An understanding of social processes typical of the socialist town helps us to locate and develop forces of production in a rational way, and to create optimum conditions for urban living.

At the present stage of construction, we urgently need to study the everyday life of the labouring classes and social groups — *i.e.*, problems associated with people's material and cultural lives. The Communist Party of the Soviet Union and the Soviet government are tackling that particular task. The Directives of the 24th CPSU Congress on the Ninth Five-Year USSR Economic Development Plan for 1971-1975 emphasised that "the main task of the five-year plan is to ensure a substantial rise in people's material and cultural standards on the basis of a high growth rate in socialist production, improved efficiency, scientific and technical progress and faster growth in labour productivity."[2] Our Party proceeds from Lenin's maxim in defining the socialist order as essentially a system of social production designed to meet people's requirements more and more fully in a planned way to achieve the all-round development of every member of society.

Research into the various aspects of urban life, particularly the living conditions of the Soviet working class, is obviously important to the social sciences; they may be able to help greatly in resolving the theoretical and practical problems that arise as we build communism. Results of research into urban life are of undoubted interest to a wide range of public organisations concerned with ideological education and to economic organisations tackling key issues in the long-term planning of housing construction and community services, in improving the essential services and leisure-time amenities of the urban population.[3] Our urban studies have so far been weak and existing literature has not provided a proper theoretical foundation for studying the problem.

The establishment and development of a new socialist urban way of life correspond to the needs of our epoch. The dialectics of these processes require thorough social analysis, a radical reconstruction of the old mode of life, an awareness of the internal workings and contradictions of the principles of contemporary urban living and of ways of forming new social relations in everyday life. The social sciences are now gathering and systematising factual material which has great significance for an understanding of general and specific questions of Soviet urban life. We should stress, however, that an analysis of individual processes can be no substitute for comprehensive, all-embracing research and a historical synthesis of extremely complicated and diverse phenomena of everyday life.

This book highlights the significance of urban life in advanced socialist society; it provides methodological and methodical principles for investigating Soviet urban life and supports them by empirical social research. It also presents information on the history of urban studies both here and abroad.

The author has not dealt exhaustively with all the problems presented. Certain major issues of urban life (health, social pathology, social psychology, etc.) are ignored while others are only touched upon superficially. To do them justice they demand specialist works based on systematic research.

Chapter 1

Methodological and Methodical Principles of Soviet Urban Sociology

Problems of everyday life occupy a central place in communist construction. Their study is fundamental to proper planning of social development; moreover, rational organisation of everyday life facilitates the all-round development of the individual.

We have so far given insufficient attention to everyday life in the towns, especially that of the leading force of Soviet society — the working class. However paradoxical it may sound, we still do not have an agreed concept of 'everyday life'. In this connection, it is interesting to compare the concepts 'way of life' and 'everyday life'; in our opinion, the concept 'way of life' is much wider and deeper than 'everyday life'. Way of life depends on the nature and level of development of the forces of production; it is made up of two closely-related fields of human endeavour: social production — *i.e.*, the labour activity of individuals — and everyday life — *i.e.*, people's lives outside production.

Changes in the nature of labour and the conditions of everyday life transform the way of life of classes, social groups and strata and create a new relationship between labour and everyday life. Under capitalism, labour and everyday life are two antipodes of human life, while, under socialism, there is no sharp contradiction, and opposition between them gradually fades away.[1] The way of life that takes shape in socialist states helps, on the other hand, to eradicate bourgeois individualistic morality and, on the other, to establish and strengthen communist morality.

On a theoretical plane there exist two points of view about everyday life which, though similar in certain respects, by no means coincide. Thus, the ethnographers L.A. Anokhina, V. Yu. Krupyanskaya and M.N. Shmeleva write: "In the wide sense, everyday life may be defined as people's day-to-day way of life based on conventional routine, traditions, established relationships and other phenomena that have taken shape during people's social (including productive) activity, their family and domestic lives. From that standpoint, it is legitimate to speak of social, productive and domestic (or, more widely, family) everyday life."[2] This is an example of a wide and even all-embracing interpretation of everyday life.

The term is more frequently formulated in a narrower sense. S. Kovalev considers that "everyday life is a social-science term reflecting the non-productive sphere of human life, directly concerned with the satisfaction of material and cultural requirements for food, clothing, dwelling and community services, health treatment and protection, leisure and entertainment."[3] A.G. Kharchev fully shares that view.[4] V.G. Sinitsyn emphasises that "everyday life is a way or form of daily life beyond the sphere of production and social activity, directly characterising the ways and means by which people satisfy their various material and cultural requirements."[5] This definition precludes both a person's productive and his social activity. B.D. Parygin takes almost the same view in examining the psychology of everyday life — *i.e.*, a principal field of applied social psychology.[6]

On the one hand, then, we have a wide interpretation of everyday life, embracing all facets of a person's life (Anokhina, Krupyanskaya and Shmeleva), and a narrow definition, on the other. In the latter instance, it is restricted merely to consumption of material and cultural benefits and is not extended to production (Kovalev, Kharchev) or to a person's social activity (Sinitsyn, Parygin).

It is not hard to discern that the all-embracing definition of everyday life which encompasses productive activity arose under the influence of ethnography which, until very recently, had concentrated primarily on the culture and everyday life of backward and poorly-developed peoples. It was quite natural to study the economic activity — *i.e.*, 'everyday productive life' — of particular tribes and peoples. But unqualified acceptance of certain propositions applicable to the study of backward tribes is quite unjustified and even mistaken in investigating modern advanced societies.[7]

In so far as work and non-productive activity constitute the basis of a person's activity in advanced socialist society, everyday life reflects both spheres. It is hard to conceive of a regime of labour-time (duration of the working day and week, rest breaks, 24-hour routine on day- and night-shifts, overtime, etc.) having no direct effect on the nature of people's lives outside their work. Everyday life is, therefore, connected with work activity and bears its imprint — *i.e.*, everyday life and production are mutually determined spheres of a single social organism.

It is quite different to apply everyday life as a phenomenon of social life to modern advanced society and confine it merely to the non-productive sphere. If we do, we must accept the idea that everyday life does not play a decisive part in the life of society, that it possesses a relative autonomy and specific laws in its development and operation. This approach does enable us to isolate the phenomenon as an independent object of study by the various individual sciences. Certainly, work has long been an object of specialist research by such disciplines as labour economics and industrial sociology.

In favour of the argument that everyday life belongs to the non-productive sphere is the fact that our widespread time-budget studies shows a clear delineation of working and non-working time. Moreover, the elements that comprise non-productive time (non-working time related to production; time for satisfying physiological needs; time spent on housework; free time) express the basic features of everyday life in a general concentrated form. Yet, at the same time, we do wish to stress that a direct and straightforward connection exists between working time and various parts of non-working time, due to a whole number of social and economic factors.

In regard to people's social activity, let us note only that we are evidently faced with a range of needs related to social conditions and unconnected directly with the sphere of everyday life, even though they exert an influence upon it.

From the foregoing we may now give the following definition of everyday life: everyday life is a day-to-day, historically-shaped way of satisfying personal material and cultural requirements which have taken shape under the influence of the traditions and customs of class, social group and nationality reinforced in the sphere of ethno-social psychology. Marxist science understands by personal consumption the major part of non-productive consumption going to satisfy the public's personal needs (food, clothing, housing, etc.). Satisfaction of cultural requirements is also an important element in the structure of personal consumption. Personal needs depend on the socio-psychological characteristics of classes, on national and ethnic features — *i.e.*, the customs, mores and historically-accumulated experience in satisfying individual consumption — and on the ideological factor which is apparent in the conscious experience which the ruling classes use to exert their influence upon the common people.

The above-mentioned definition therefore has the advantage that everyday life belongs equally to production and social activity, which permits it to be applied to the basic categories of historical materialism.

The historical sciences (including ethnography) treat needs as a category acting as a form rather than a measure of its own manifestation, while the economic sciences study needs as a category of living standards — *i.e.*, as an average amount of satisfaction of needs for material and cultural benefits that has taken shape at a given historical stage. It is the task of sociology here, in our view, to investigate the functioning both of the forms and of the measure of the needs of a social individual. Economic and sociological literature has recently confirmed the wide interpretation of standard of living, by which we should understand the amount and measure of satisfying growing material and cultural needs. Thus, the task of the sociologist or economist here is to investigate factors that bring the standard of living into line as much as possible with the capacity of socialist society for maintaining and raising it.

Some tasks are beyond the grasp of the economist or sociologist. We refer to the individual nature of the process, the discovery of its specific forms manifest in specific historical circumstances that reflect regional, ethnic and other peculiarities. Consequently, we have to study the historical uniqueness of the way living standards function with their own conceptual apparatus. This does not find wide application either in economics or in sociology. In this case, everyday life may be a category of historical science. Everyday life, like living standards, depends on social relations and social structure, is an attribute of them and alters as society develops.

Bearing in mind that everyday life is a relatively conservative phenomenon which lags behind social, political and economic change, we can uncover the many processes occurring in everyday life in a profound and comprehensive way only by being historically consistent, even if the nature of the research is not historical. True, we can only apply a historical approach to everyday life through a thorough sociological analysis of the given phenomenon. There is, obviously, no genuine historicism outside of scientific sociology.

To sum up, in all work on improving everyday life we need a specific historical approach, a really scientific consideration of economic, social and cultural circumstances and all the difficulties and contradictions that arise.

Thanks to our enormous economic progress, public welfare is steadily improving and the ever mounting material and cultural needs are being met. This is bettering everyday life and greatly facilitating the formation of an all-round developed and harmonious personality — the builder of communism. As the size and structure of national wealth change today, the basis of communist everyday life takes shape and a new morality emerges; this has a beneficial effect in transforming the entire life-style of a Soviet person. We have established a new lifestyle in our country, developing on a single social basis and "connected with public socialist ownership and socialist production. It is founded on social and national equality, on the equality of men and women, on comradely mutual assistance and on the collective surmounting of all difficulties. That is the prime social result of changes to everyday life during the Soviet years."[8]

Under capitalism, the way of life of diametrically-opposed, antagonistic classes is contradictory in the extreme. Socialism, however, precludes any extreme differentiation in life-styles. But it does not remove completely the differences in living standards of the various social groups, differences that emanate from the present state of the economy; a certain unequal distribution of gross national product, which has an objective basis, remains for some time. Both class and certain social distinctions within classes themselves remain at the present stage of the development of forces and relations of production. Hence the importance of studying everyday life in the context of the social structure of classes and individual groups. Furthermore, it is important to pay special attention to everyday-life differences within the working class, the peasants and the intellectuals based on occupational groups.

We attribute great importance to social structure as a factor affecting the organisation of everyday life and share the view of G.V. Osipov and S.F. Frolov when they emphasise that "not only do social living conditions determine human behaviour; man himself selects from all the material and cultural conditions of his social milieu those which best correspond to his individual qualities and express those qualities objectively."[9] They are talking, in effect, about individual everyday life which may be compared to other forms of everyday life.

To understand everyday life fully we need to make a careful analysis of material living conditions, the extent of satisfaction of cultural needs, family relationships and other relations between people in the non-productive sphere. Research into such problems should be based on overall social conditions, their specific forms and multi-faceted relations. It cannot be made in isolation. To comprehend family relationships, for example, helps us to elucidate many other features of everyday life which, in turn, allows us to evaluate the various processes and trends that occur within the family. Such an approach brings us also to an understanding of social, urban, rural and individual everyday life.

It is apparent from the above-mentioned issues which are part of everyday life that we need to employ in the research several interrelated social sciences: sociology, economics, history, ethnography, etc. The problem is indeed at the cross-roads of several sciences in every sense. We may therefore use the vast store of information which each discipline contains; that should give the most tangible, meaningful results in any work devoted to everyday life.

Interest in everyday life arose in the latter part of the last century. In tracing its historiography in the broad sense, we may refer primarily to the classics of Marxism-Leninism who paid a great deal of attention to the living conditions of the working class.

In Chapter 23 of *Capital*, Karl Marx revealed the general law of capitalist accumulation and described in some detail the everyday living conditions of the industrial proletariat.[10] Using statistics and numerous documents, he scrupulously analysed the wages, food, housing conditions, cultural standards and other aspects of the lives of English workers in the years 1840-1860. Marx combined a profound scientific analysis of the vast material with lively and graphic pictures of the then everyday lives of the working class.

Friedrich Engels in his book *The Condition of the Working Classes in England in 1844-1845* and in *On the Housing Question*, published 27 years later, examined closely the material welfare and cultural standards of the working class, presenting a vivid picture of life in the big capitalist cities.[11] To complete his work, Engels had to unearth and examine a vast number of sources, using a comprehensive approach to gather the data he needed.

Vladimir Lenin's book *The Development of Capitalism in Russia* is a classic example of a thorough scientific analysis of the everyday life of workers at the end of the last century. He clearly indicates his methodological principles in studying cash earnings, income-expenditure accounts in worker-families and other aspects of everyday life that took shape as Russian capitalism rapidly developed. He highlighted the low living standards of workers and saw this as "the most acute difference between the incomes of *boss* and *worker*."[12]

These and other Marxist-Leninist works today have great methodological significance in tackling the problem of the everyday life of Soviet people. The methods used should depend on the purposes of the research and on the general methodological precepts of historical materialism. Researchers are faced by several procedural questions: they must select a research subject, adopt the best method of observing and gathering primary material, then prepare it for quantitative processing and qualitative analysis.

An objective and exact study of the features of everyday life can only be based on comprehensive methods. Hence the need for making full use of several existing methods:

(i)   analysis of already published documentary sources;
(ii)   questionnaires, interviews and tests;
(iii)   acquaintance with personal documents (letters, diaries, etc.);
(iv)   expert evaluation;
(v)   free conversation and personal observation;
(vi)   social experimenting, etc.

Each of these methods has its advantages in regard to specific problems. But, as we have stressed, only a comprehensive approach using all these methods will enable the researcher to understand fully such a complicated and multi-faceted phenomenon as everyday life.

The quantitative method is important in that it can elicit many features of everyday life and other social demographic data necessary for analysing people's everyday lives. It should not be used exclusively because qualitative analysis is also of prime importance in the social sciences.

As Soviet and foreign experience shows, the object of study may be a large factory, a group of factories, a housing estate, a city district or an entire town. Choice of object must be completely justified and based on research objectives.

In preparing independent research, much attention must be paid to compiling a proper programme for gathering material and determining stages of investigation and selection so that the resultant data are sufficiently representative.[13] This often presents difficulties because our statistical agencies do not provide information on several factors concerning everyday life (information on families by size, for example). It is also recommended to make a trial, exploratory survey to test the programme and validity of the assembled research tools. In certain instances, the investigation should be preceded by preliminary interviews with persons within the sample survey; this helps test the hypotheses, since the more we know of the object we are investigating, the greater the probability that we have formulated correct premises.

Much depends here, of course, on the complexity of the hypotheses. A simple hypothesis may quite often produce automatic answers to the questions set. In testing hypotheses, careful account must be taken of the relationship between various indices; moreover, it is important to establish their dimension in relation to one another so as to test the specific relations between the objects of study.

The material obtained by independent research must be subjected to systematic testing and re-testing so as to exclude chance and to highlight the most essential and typical features of the object of study. The researcher should therefore take into consideration contradictions inherent in phenomena and not rely only upon facts favourable to the initial viewpoint. Therein lies the basic distinction between the work of Soviet scholars based on Marxist-Leninist methodology and that of bourgeois scholars who normally take an empirical approach without stating — even completely divorced from — general theoretical and methodological problems.

We may investigate everyday life by a method revealing the principal features of everyday life (material, cultural, family, etc.) or by the cumulative method (according to household inventory, time-budgets, etc.). These research methods facilitate study of the structure of everyday life from the standpoint of the relationship between:

(a) its public and individual aspects;

(b) types of activity associated with them;

(c) the different forms of human association and contact in this sphere of social life.

We only have space to mention the importance of time-budget studies. They can reflect major aspects of everyday life and serve as a prime source for creating a clear picture of a live situation which would enable us optimally to combine material and cultural needs in everyday life. Furthermore, analysis of the time-fund gives us an idea of the structure of everyday life which makes it possible to understand more profoundly the essence of urban life and to provide a thorough analysis of the causal connections between all aspects of the problem.

The great popularity of time-budget studies in sociology is in no small measure due to the fact that the theoretical premises and hypotheses lend themselves to testing — *i.e.*, the interrelationship between theoretical and empirical research is patently clear. Moreover, time-budgets enable us to uncover those aspects of people's lives which cannot be considered directly using natural and value indices. This is obtained by using a system consisting of time indices in combination with demographic and social characteristics of the individual. This quality of time-budgets makes it possible to establish the overall trends of social development, many patterns of work, everyday life and leisure, to comprehend the interrelationship between society and the individual, and to pinpoint certain causal factors in the traits of a harmoniously developed personality.

G.S. Petrosyan rightly stresses that the nature and organisation of everyday life "very directly influence the structure of use of non-working time. Changes in the nature and organisation of everyday life invariably lead to changes in the structure of utilisation of non-working time and vice versa."[14] The specific nature of non-working time — *i.e.*, the concentrated expression of everyday life as a creative process affecting all aspects of an individual's life — may be understood only by using a Marxist approach to working time as a determinant of non-working time. The interrelationship between these concepts is not free of certain contradictions despite their apparent simplicity.

Soviet social science now possesses, mainly thanks to the work of G.A. Prudensky[15], a strong methodological foundation for time-budget studies, a clear time-fund structure and its classification into the following basic groups:

1. Working Time
(i) Actual work (contracted and overtime);
(ii) Time wasted and non-productive working time;
(iii) Official work breaks;
(iv) Shift change-over.

2. Non-Working Time
(i) Time related to work in production (moving to and from the workplace, time for personal needs before and after the shift, etc);

(ii) Time devoted to housework and everyday domestic needs (shopping, cooking, child-care, laundry, other household work, etc.);

(iii) Time devoted to physiological needs — *i.e.*, sleeping and eating;

(iv) Free time spent on study, improving qualifications, self-education, social work*, rest, leisure, etc.;

(v) Other time expenditure.

This classification is particularly valuable in that it enables us to judge the magnitude of working and non-working time, and to understand their interrelationship and the ways to increase free time.

Analysis reveals that less working time has a direct effect on more free time. A more rational use of the non-working time structure is a no less important reserve for augmenting free time.

The total time-fund structure cannot be uniform and unalterable because it depends, first, on the principles that underlie its construction and, secondly, on the differences in the nature and types of activity in the working and non-working time of various categories of people (workers, employees, collective farmers, etc.) and of population groups. Further, the nature of people's activity in working and non-working time undergoes certain changes as society develops.

Time-budget studies according to elements of time expenditure, when the entire time (daily, weekly, monthly, etc.) is neatly classified into working and non-working time, are widely recognised; their methodological principles have been tried and tested in numerous experiments both at home and abroad in socialist and capitalist countries.[16] With this approach, time-budgets are usually studied through a single member of a family within the sample.

P.P. Maslov takes a different view of time-budget studies;[17] he is opposed to the studying of them on the basis of the time-expenditure of a single family member. Instead, he suggests studying the overall family time-balance rather than an individual time-budget.[18] In our opinion, both these methodological premises do not preclude one another and may be used separately or together depending on the research objectives. Maslov, incidentally, put forward only a hypothetical viewpoint still unconfirmed by extensive concrete social research. But his views are obviously attractive, even though it is hard to agree with him that the principles of time-budget studies are equivalent to those of a family's consumpt-

---

* Social work includes giving lectures, attending meetings, conferences, etc., electoral functions, work in 'public order squads' (*e.g.*, traffic control), working on commissions and doing a variety of gratuitous jobs (see V.A. Artemov, et al., *Statistika byudzhetov vremeni trudyashchikhsya*, Moscow, 1966, p. 189) [*JR*].

ion-budgets. This approach is deficient because income distribution and time-fund allocation within a family are obviously not the same. In the latter instance we must consider not only economic necessity determined by the family's economic function, but also a variety of traditions, standards and stereotypes of value orientations and judgements in the minds of individual family members, and other social factors.

A new typology of free time based on multiple analysis has recently appeared.[19] It constructs a time-expenditure typology, using the type-recognition method. The authors of this method made up a typology of the non-working time of a group of workers at different factories, distinguishing such types of time-expenditure as 'family-cultural', 'study-cultural', 'harmonious', and so on. While not dwelling in detail on this methodological approach, let us note that it merits consideration and may be improved in subsequent investigations, including those concerned with the everyday life of towndwellers.

To understand everyday life properly and comprehensively, it is vital to have information on an aggregate time-budget whose structure may serve both as a basis for theoretical conclusions on various social processes in everyday life and for applied studies intended to explain, for example, the daily procedure in different types of family. We tend not to use time-budget material widely in nearly all works specifically on everyday life.

Another central issue in regard to everyday life is that of free time. On the amount of free time, we can decide ways and means of satisfying the cultural, moral and aesthetic needs of the individual, social group, class or society. By free time we understand that part of non-working time that goes to a person's physical and cultural development, and to his leisure; according to the more succinct definition given by B.A. Grushin, it is "time free from performing any urgent obligations."[20] An analysis of free time helps us understand the structure of an individual's activity related to his occupational group, demographic characteristics, etc.

In this context, let us note that while our sociologists and economists agree on how to distinguish non-working from free time, they are still not clear about whether 'free time' is identical with 'leisure'. A work expressly devoted to time-budgets provides an exhaustive analysis of classification of non-working time elements (related to the ways that needs are satisfied, degree of rational expenditure, etc.)[21], but ignores the question of the relationship between the concepts 'free time' and 'leisure'.

Grushin, who examines the problem of free time proper in his book, considers the two concepts identical.[22] Yet, other authors think differently.[23]

We agree with the latter in believing that the concept 'free time' is much wider than that of 'leisure'. On the one hand, it includes *socially-necessary creative endeavour* (study, self-education and improving qualifications, social activity) and the performance of certain family functions (involvement with children). On the other hand, it encompasses the remainder of free time which a person spends exclusively by his own choice and inclinations – *i.e.*, *leisure* (enjoying cultural benefits, engaging in physical culture and games, work-hobbies, meeting friends and relations, various forms of passive leisure and so-called undistributed time).[24] We may recall that Marx once said of free time that it was both time for leisure and time for improving oneself.[25] We believe it unjustified, therefore, to include time for study, social work and, especially, everyday domestic needs in the concept 'leisure'. But it should encompass time spent on improving cultural standards — reading general political literature and fiction, listening to the radio, watching television and attending lectures.[26]

A correct delineation of 'free time' and 'leisure' makes it easier theoretically to internalise the problem of leisure which is closely bound up with social macro-structures and other phenomena related to modern urban living.

While the construction of aggregate time-budgets provides and understanding of the way of life and everyday life as a whole, we can understand the essence of leisure by examining free time; the total amount of leisure tells us how we can best satisfy people's social, cultural, moral and aesthetic needs, their rest-time and physical development.

Leisure is a form of creative or passive activity which is not part of a person's day-to-day vital obligations. Clearly, we cannot make a hard and fast distinction between a person's socially-necessary creative endeavour and his leisure. Reading, for instance, may serve the purpose of self-education or simply be a means of passing the time. Meanwhile, the nature of leisure cannot be free of the existing social and economic conditions, despite its sphere of activity belonging to an informal structure which is not circumscribed so strictly as the work sphere.

The great variety of and improvement in forms of leisure are primarily due to the growth in towns and to large-scale industrial production; it is therefore quite valid to talk of contemporary leisure as a phenomenon which is continually changing and developing in the process of urbanisation. Only in the era of the industrial revolution and scientific progress has the urban population, for the most part, been able to enjoy such a large amount of free time. This was impossible in earlier historical periods because of the low level of economic development. In the final analysis, leisure is determined by the economic system and social factors operating within a particular socio-economic formation. A Marxist approach to the problem of leisure exposes the fallacious assertions of bourgeois scholars, like A.W. Green, who believe that leisure is creating the modern way of life[27] or, like M. Kaplan, who views leisure as the antithesis of work.[28] Many other bourgeois writers take an anti-Marxist position in their approach to leisure.[29]

The nature of leisure can only be understood by comprehending the theoretical meaning of work and non-work activity, their mutual impact upon one another. Hence, leisure should be understood as a phenomenon cognisable through the interrelationship between the time a person spends in productive life and the time he devotes to non-productive life. As a process, however, leisure enters into time that is free from work. (True, leisure probably includes, too, that small amount of time which a person may spend on intellectual development during work breaks.)

It is hard to exaggerate the importance of leisure in the overall structure of contemporary everyday life. An analysis of the specific meaning of leisure enables us to comprehend ways and means of satisfying the public's cultural needs. Reconstruction of everyday life along socialist lines alters the nature of leisure and this, in turn, affects the formation of completely new features of everyday life. Leisure is a criterion of the cultural outlook of an individual, social group or society as a whole; meaningless use of leisure-time slows down the progressive movement of society. Leisure affects both the personality and the social structure of contemporary society. Hence the need to keep in constant touch with public opinion so as to be able to use the ever-increasing amount of free time in a rational way. Organised leisure, if it is based on the interests of society and the individual, safeguards the public from many instances of social disorganisation and personal demoralisation.[30]

Leisure is today the basis of mankind's cultural attainments. It is therefore inhumane and reactionary for some bourgeois writers to make pessimistic claims that there is a 'leisure crisis'[31] or that the increasing free time at the disposal of many working people, particularly the working class, represents a grave danger to mankind.[32] Understandably, the problem of leisure, like that of free time generally, presupposes a different approach under capitalism and socialism; we have to take account of the specific nature of various social phenomena and locate them in definite social reality. With such a class-partisan approach, we can discern the nature of and radical distinctions between leisure in socialist and capitalist states.[33]

There is no uniformity in using free time. Any form of leisure may give satisfaction to one person and be boring to another. Furthermore, some types of leisure may constitute work or entertainment for the same person at different times (a hunter, for example, may go about his job professionally or simply be a sportsman). Although a person is under the control and influence of a dominant ideology, social affiliation and set habits, the meaning of leisure may often be more clearly manifest in regard to the personality than to social factors.

Elements of leisure come partly under the sway of past traditions and partly under the influence of the on-going scientific revolution and, in some instances, of other forces operating beyond the direct control of society. We see here most clearly features of the complex and indirect effort of the social milieu and the entire society upon people with their specific and individual qualities, which ultimately form the multi-faceted and diverse structure of people's interests.

A person's life cannot be treated wholly in terms of the past, present or future. His creative endeavour is based on all three. So we cannot view leisure merely as a phenomenon determined by time-expenditure; it has to be seen in a wider context as progressive restoration and newly-replenished content. Leisure today is affected both by the increasingly technical urbanisation-process and by the overall situation that has taken shape historically in a particular country or area. We can perceive the relationship between the values of industrial and pre-industrial society in the various elements of leisure.

A certain type of leisure takes shape under the influence of many factors: geographical, ecological, demographic, political, social and economic organisation. Its specific form depends greatly on sex, age, education and social affiliation. Evidently, leisure makes a major contribution to eliminating class and social distinctions — *i.e.*, to creating a socially-homogeneous society.

From the foregoing it is apparent that leisure is of great importance in the entire complex sphere of everyday life. The family is indisputably the main form of social contact in everyday life; but, in organising and engaging in leisure, other forms of association and contact are important, such as clubs, workingmen's associations and informal groups.

Understanding the actual nature of leisure helps us to discern the features of social, family and individual leisure, and their interaction. When we speak of individual leisure, we have in mind an individual's ability to choose his leisure; this gives us an insight into the relationship between personal values and those of society.

Finally, science is playing an increasing part in transforming everyday life, for socialism opens up substantial opportunities for arranging everyday life on a scientific basis; that, in the final count, helps considerably to raise living standards in town and country. There lies the topical importance of research which propounds new hypotheses from which we may understand the relationship between variables, their verification and the formulation on their basis of particular patterns shaped by development and changes in everyday life. Parallel with this, we have to develop scientific forecasting and modelling of the principal components of everyday life over long periods.

Intensified research in this field would be of more than purely academic interest; it could be useful in improving urban life and exposing the fallacies of bourgeois scholars who frequently distort Soviet living conditions.

Chapter 2

From the History of Urban Studies in the USSR and Abroad

1. Soviet urban studies

There were no systematic urban studies in pre-revolutionary Russia. Individual works existed which largely summarised results of research into workers' consumption patterns[1] and certain other issues.[2]

Extensive urban studies only developed after the revolution. Even then the research was not comprehensive because it focused attention only on industrial workers. By the mid-1920's, serious works appeared which merit attention for their approach to the problems and methods they used to study the everyday lives of the working class — the leading force of Soviet society.

One of the first researchers into the everyday life of Soviet workers was S.G. Strumilin. His publications of the mid-1920's contain valuable theoretical propositions and detailed statistical and economic information on may aspects of workers' lives. He went considerably further than the small band of his predecessors. In his work *Towards a Methodology of a Worker's Budget,* published in 1924, he writes the following: "Budget research is today of much wider and deeper significance than it has ever been in the past. It should serve us to resolve a whole number of practical problems in economic planning. From the budgets we can study the capacity of our market, the burden of taxation, the speed of currency circulation and many other, just as practical, vital specialist issues, not to mention its use in constructing a nation-wide economic balance with which we may underpin all planning proposals and calculations for the future. In view of this, the methodology of budget-studies goes beyond the bounds of purely academic considerations."[3]

In the above-mentioned work, Strumilin puts forward interesting views on gathering and processing workers' income budgets which, from a methodological respect — and this is worth emphasising — are just as valid today. Basing himself on the experience accumulated at that time, he rejected the questionnaire-method of compiling budgets and that of recording the day-to-day income-expenditure account for families in the study. He based his objections on the generally low cultural level then prevailing. Talking of the workers themselves filling in questionnaires, Strumilin stressed that "only the most literate among them can cope with this properly, but day-to-day records demand, naturally, an even higher cultural level than with a single instance of filling in forms. The atypical nature of material collected in this manner is pre-guaranteed."[4]

He thought the bext method of investigating workers' budgets was the follow-up expeditionary survey which had to be combined, or backed up, with specific day-to-day records. He proposed paring the investigation period to the minimum — to a week, for example — so as to conduct follow-up investigations at a different time of the year. That method, as Strumilin rightly claimed, is also useful in enabling the research-supervisor to have direct contact with the worker at home, in his family surroundings, which enables him to test and verify various statements. In that way, Strumilin substantiated the representative nature of the material collected.

He relied, further, on such propositions as the transfer-factor, the homogeneity of comparable groups and the principles of grouping different variables that distinguish the worker's welfare — *i.e.*, he laid down fundamental principles which no modern researcher into urban worker studies can ignore.

Strumilin raised interesting theoretical questions in his other publications, assembled under the general title *To a Study of the Everyday Life of Working People in the USSR.*[5] Here he stressed the political significance of research into everyday life which had undergone drastic changes: in the whole tenor of life and the outlook of the worker-family. Strumilin maintained that everyday life should be the focus of attention of trade unions — *i.e.*, he posed the vital question of the link between worker-studies and the practical work of trade-union organisations.

It should be pointed out that Strumilin did his detailed worker-studies not only on money-[6] and time-budgets, not yet depicting, in his words, "the material environment of everyday life"; he also made a careful study of available household inventories.[7] Study of the 'itemised' inventory of everyday life gives an idea of the worker's welfare and cultural level and certain other aspects that do not lend themselves to examination by other methods.

It is today virtually impossible to find worker-studies that do not use material borrowed from Strumilin's works. That is all the more significant since, in 1961, he correlated his research results of the 1920's with analogous data from 1959.[8]

Y.O. Kabo was another of the pioneer researchers into workers' everyday life in the 1920's. In 1926, she published a work on the food consumption of a Russian worker before and after World War I.[9] On the basis of her concrete statistical data, she showed that by late 1924 Russian workers were eating more and better, on many indices, than before the war. By that time, too, workers' wages had risen (particularly in Moscow and Leningrad) and domestic food prices had fallen (in 1923 they were, for example, only 44.3 per cent of the pre-war Petrograd figure).[10] Kabo was also able to outline "the way in which workers' consumption should and could improve given constantly rising wages: by lower-paid workers increasing their consumption of dearer foodstuffs — *i.e.*, by reducing differentiation"[11] between different strata of workers.

We must add that Kabo calculated food expenditure according to Engel's law which has the major deficiency that its food-consumption scale takes only age and sex into consideration.[12] She did concede that the proposed Engel formula, in which food expenditure depends exclusively on the income level of a worker's family, was borne out only in the expenditure side of the budget, going to the consumption of the "cheaper and least elastic foodstuffs."

Kabo brought out another book in 1928 which dealt with the everyday life of Moscow workers.[13] She confined herself here to studying domestic life selecting the family as observation unit — *i.e.*, the most typical form of domestic life. She provided a basically correct definition of a family as a small social group distinguished by a set of biological, juridical, economic and regional features.[14] But her formula lacked socio-historical causality of familial organisation, which is a crucial component in family relations.

Kabo noticed the tendency for large families to decline and for small family units to predominate in a worker-household. From a detailed study of 62 families, she revealed the social status of workers and classified them by their life-style. She showed that everyday life essentially depended upon social origin, material and cultural habits acquired by the family from the milieu from which it had sprung, wage-level — the basis of economic welfare — and the social and political conditions prevailing in the USSR. It is to her credit that she indicated the beginnings of the new life, the transformation of everyday life under the impact of the new Soviet school, cultural institutions and the immense organisational work of the Communist Party and the Komsomol.

The information Kabo collected on material living conditions of workers (housing, clothing, food, etc.) may serve as a reliable historical source even today. We can also learn something from the methods she employed in studying the everyday life of Moscow workers. Besides statistical data, she relied on material obtained by direct observation often of the same subject over quite a long period. She defined correctly the prime functions of the worker-family and showed how living conditions in 1924-25 had improved since before 1917. Without enumerating many other merits of her work, let us state simply that besides reflecting truly the everyday life of a worker-family, she also indicated contradictions in everyday life at a time when the mounting material and cultural needs could not be met in full because of the low economic level of the young Soviet Republic.

A collective work was published in 1930 on the lives of young workers at the Karl Marx Engineering Works in Leningrad.[15] It described aspects of the cultural and everyday life of young workers at one of Leningrad's largest factories. The authors noted that many workers (59.5 per cent) at the works were uneducated, even at a level of five classes (at that time the target was for young people to have a seven-year elementary school education). Yet, even then, many young workers were supplementing their general education or studying at various vocational schools and trainee-enterprises. It is remarkable that so few girls were involved in vocational training. Alongside the growth in healthy cultural demands, there persisted strong adverse phenomena such as sexual promiscuity and excessive consumption of spirits.

This work might well be the basis for a fresh analogous study at the Karl Marx Works in order to trace the changes that have taken place in the cultural outlook of young workers over the ensuing 40 years.

S. Lapitskaya published a book in 1935 on the everyday life of workers at one of Moscow's biggest mills — the *Tryokhgornaya manufaktura*.[16] The value of the work lies in the fact that Lapitskaya studied life under serfdom, capitalism and socialist construction. She portrayed clearly the break with the old and the affirmation of the new way of life which took shape as socialism was being built. Interestingly enough, besides archive documents and literary sources, she made extensive use of information obtained through *ad hoc* surveys conducted jointly by mill-workers and research workers.

During the 1920's considerable investigation was made into the psychology of everyday life.[17] Scholars paid much attention to concrete research into psychological features of everyday life: feelings, moods, customs and other stable and mobile components of a worker's social psychology. They employed a variety of methods in investigating everyday life and worker-psychology, and the social causes of the various social phenomena, relying on observation techniques and analysis of documents. It is remarkable that D. Lebdev and M. Rafail published an original work using material from wall-newspapers and letters from worker-correspondents. At the request of the editors of *Rabochaya gazeta (Workers' Newspaper)*, for example, Lebedev examined 16,000 such letters on over 400 themes. Within the confines of a small brochure, he attempted to convey (and his efforts were, in our view, successful) the mood of the workers and their active involvement in building the new life.

From the mid-1920's to the early 1930's, statistical handbooks were printed containing vast factual material on the structure of everyday life of manual workers and, partly, of employees too.[18] The date contained in these publications showed the dynamic growth in the material prosperity and cultural standards of worker-families during that period; they also give a picture of the family income, housing conditions, furniture and household equipment, clothing, food, cultural level and so on. Some of them contained worker time-budget studies, so making it possible to know and consciously affest the changes taking place in the lives of workers, especially in non-working time.

To investigate everyday life requires a good grasp of the question of living standards. Here we must dwell briefly on works devoted to this salient issue.

Two articles appeared in the 1930's on living standards.[19] M. Krivitsky studied methodical principles which could be applied to studying the living standards of manual workers. He also described different approaches to these issues in regard to workers in the USSR and in capitalist states. He justly criticised bourgeois scholars for frequently confining themselves to investigating living standards only on the basis of income (individual and family) and movement in the cost of living index. Such an approach narrows the problem and excludes a whole number of vital indices without which it is impossible to gain a proper understanding of workers' living standards. Besides examining budget structure which, too, should be studied dynamically, Krivitsky proposed considering the following factors: the nature and conditions of work, unemployment, the involvement of women and children in production, the everyday-life situation, the number and employment of members of the worker-family, overall literacy, death rate, life and health protection of those working and, finally, the share of the working class in national income.

Proceeding from the principle that living standards depended on a specific socio-economic structure, Krivitsky focused attention on the supplementary means received by the Soviet worker from public funds. The expenditure-structure of public funds therefore consisted of the following indices:

    (i)   social insurance benefits;
    (ii)   trade-union benefits;
    (iii)   student grants;
    (iv)   education and cultural services;
    (v)   health service;
    (vi)   everyday-life improvement fund.

Krivitsky pointed out that in Soviet conditions it was wrong to look solely at wages and public funds. It was necessary to take account of the nature and intensity of labour, length of the working day, the proportion of female labour and abolition of child labour in industry, the lack of unemployment,etc. He frequently stressed the importance of studying the conditions of everyday life, particularly the housing problem and housework. He correctly posed the question of involving women in work and promoting public catering, children's institutions, etc. Finally, he made a special plea for analysing worker time-budgets as a crucial index supplementing other data.

Krivitsky's scheme does not invite serious objections, although we cannot agree with his inclusion in everyday life only of density and data on new house-building, while excluding such a major component as health protection. Clearly, he did not have a precise understanding of the concept 'everyday life'; hence his extreme lack of clarity in formulating its components.

The article by S. Heinman does not deal with theoretical issues but it does contain factual material that sheds light on living standards in the 1930's not only of workers, but of peasants and working intellectuals as well. The author highlights the sharp rise in living standards due to agricultural reconstruction through the collective- and state-farm system.

Time-budgets that give a concentrated picture of everyday life are vital sources for a profound study of the lives of Soviet workers. Such work enables us, for example, to trace changes in the lives of workers from different occupational groups and to note improvements in their cultural and technical standards.

S.G. Strumilin was the first to make a comprehensive study of time-budgets back in the 1920's, summarising his observations in *The Everyday Life of a Worker in Figures* and *A Time-Budget of Manual Workers in 1923-24*.[20] He made a strong appeal for a comprehensive survey of non-working time and optimum use of 'free' hours — *i.e.*, an issue which had never been posed before then.[21] Even at that time, Strumilin was drawing attention to the need to mechanise and rationalise housework by socialising the main housework jobs. Interestingly enough, the concrete material on worker time-budgets in Strumilin's works is being widely utilised today as a source that gives an insight into the everyday life of Russian workers in the 1920's.

Time-budget studies were less popular during the 1930's than they had been in the preceding period. But the decade did see the appearance of V. Mikheyev's book devoted to time-budgets of workers in Moscow and the Moscow region,[22] and the collective work of V. Lebedev-Pateiko, G. Ravinovich and D. Rodin which examined time-budgets of Leningrad workers.[23]

Just a few observations on the theoretical value of these works. V. Mikheyev divided the whole time-budget into the following parts: work, meals, rest, sleep and undistributed time. He included in 'work' all productive labour (including housework, shopping and travel to and from the workplace) and work in looking after oneself and one's family, everyday domestic needs and social activity. This classification, first, does not divide the budget into working and non-working time and, secondly, mistakenly includes under a single 'working-time' rubric time spent on housework and travel to work and back. Finally, the material on which Mikheyev relied was based only on a small number of observations.

The authors of the second work conducted an interesting survey on worker-families in Leningrad. The research was sponsored by the Research Institute of Communal and Housing Services and Construction and the Leningrad City Executive Committee. The authors stated their targets as being to obtain material which could be used for improving housing and communal services. This was therefore one of the first studies to be undertaken expressly for economic purposes. The material provides an insight into many aspects of the everyday life of Leningrad workers in the 1930's.[24]

The above-mentioned everyday-life studies of Soviet workers in the 1924-37 period testify to the extensive scope of such research. Several of their methodological premises retain their validity today and may serve as a valuable research tool for social scientists studying everyday life.

Many writers, particularly Strumilin, clearly realised that an analysis of individual processes is no substitute for comprehensive research, a historical synthesis of complex and multi-faceted phenomena of everyday life. The works we have mentioned bring us automatically to the conclusion that problems of urban life lie at the junction of a number of sciences (history, economics, sociology, etc.). Moreover, careful acquaintance with this early research, notably that of Strumilin, suggests that it is possible to study everyday life according to its main aspects (material, cultural, etc.) and according to synthetic, general indices (time-budgets, household inventory).

In subsequent years, works on the everyday life of workers, as of other sections of the urban population, virtually ceased to be published. Articles and monographs dealing with particular problems of Soviet urban life only began to appear in the latter part of the 1950's.

We have already mentioned that living standards are closely interrelated with everyday life and constitute its economic foundation. Therefore, it was unquestionably a healthy sign for urban studies to see the re-appearance of works on material welfare. We may cite the works of several economists and statisticians[25] dealing with welfare and Soviet consumption standards of foodstuffs and industrial commodities. They also paid some attention to methods of calculating the consumption fund. In modern urban studies, such publications may be reliable sources that contain, *inter alia*, valuable comparative historical material.

The book by P.S. Mstislavsky[26] is worthy of attention because he elaborated several methodological questions and analysed basic consumption processes and problems of improving welfare by providing sufficient housing, clothing, furniture and household equipment, food and cultural amenities.

Econometric works have appeared in recent years analysing consumption patterns and calculating real incomes of town-dwellers.[27] Some historians have also studied the material welfare of Soviet people.[28] The last decade has also seen attention focused on the Soviet working class — the leading social and political force of Soviet society. It is noteworthy that industrial workers first surpassed all other classes in 1959. The growth in the working class has continued: industrial workers constituted 48.2 per cent of the Soviet population in 1959 and 54.8 per cent in 1969.[29]

Soviet ethnographers have also made a notable contribution to working-class studies. They have combined the traditional ethnographic method of field observation with sociological analysis. Ethnographic research into the everyday life of industrial workers is in progress in many of our Union and Autonomous republics, and a great deal of work has been published on the theme.[30]

The range of topics encompassed by Soviet ethnographers in studying everyday life and culture is extremely wide. It includes the formation and current composition of industrial workers, working conditions, material welfare, the ideology and cultural outlook of the modern worker. These ethnographic works are normally concerned with contemporary themes and take account of social relations in their entirety. In the Union and Autonomous republics, where the national composition of workers is often diverse, a study of ethnic processes taking place among workers is of particular importance.

In regard to methods of work, ethnographers rely primarily on personal observation, but they also gather valuable material from archives, current documents and a wide variety of publications.[31] A marked similarity of approach between certain ethnographers and sociologists has emerged of late in urban studies.[32]

Ethnographers have recently launched a wide-ranging study of modern urban life. The pioneers were L.A. Anokhin and M.N. Shmelev who have already published their initial findings.[33] They seek a firm place for ethnographic science in contemporary urban studies, and their initial steps convince us that ethnographers, too, employing their traditional methods, may make a considerable contribution to the study of highly-urbanised contemporary society.

Sociological research has forged ahead in recent years. Yet here, too, there is so far no special work devoted to the everyday life of towndwellers, although interesting and substantive material on certain aspects of urban life has been forthcoming from research on other problems.

A.G. Zdravomyslov, V.P. Rozhin and V.A. Yadov have drawn attention to the effect on work of the extent of harmony in everyday life and in the cultural life of manual workers and of engineering and technical personnel.[34] Labour productivity would appear to rise when the conditions of everyday life of industrial workers are well arranged. Their book helps us to appreciate that everyday life, along with economic, scientific, technological and ideological factors, stimulates optimum conditions for improving the lives of Soviet people. Approximately the same range of topics on urban life is covered in other works related to industrial sociology.[35]

Some sociological works deal with changes in marriage and the family[36] and the demographic processes[37] in the urban environment. A.G. Kharchev, for example, has brought a vast amount of material to bear on such vital issues, directly affecting everyday life, as the structure and nature of intra-family relations in the modern urban family. One impressive aspect of his book *Marriage and the Family in the USSR* is that he shows himself to be the first Soviet sociologist to combine a general sociological Marxist theory of family relations with concrete sociological findings.

G.A. Slesarev's work is concerned with methodological problems of the Soviet population; he also goes into questions about changing urban living standards, the status of women and the birth-rate factor in worker-families. Many of his conclusions and ideas are based on a sample survey he conducted in Gorky among female workers in 1962. In his description of the socialist population law in practice, he rightly makes the point that "differences in the birth rate of social groups in the population are due to the different levels of needs, to the extent to which they are met, to the different living standards of these groups, their working and living conditions, life aspirations and social ideals."[38] Evidently, everyday life must be one of the principal indices determining the level of the natural movement of the urban population.[39]

Somewhat later, G.A. Slesarev and Z.A. Yankova looked at the questions of the working woman and the woman's role in the family. They also examined the everyday life of working women through interviews held in Moscow, Leningrad and Penza,[40] paying particular attention to the level of material welfare, housekeeping, allocation of jobs within the family, etc. Their conclusions are noteworthy because they raise the key and topical issue of the need to reconstruct everyday life in two directions simultaneously: improving communal services, – *i.e.*, industrialising everyday life – and 'small-scale mechanisation' – *i.e.*, providing more household appliances and labour-saving devices. The authors also appeal for change that takes the psychological factor into consideration.

Kharchev and S.I. Golod look at similar questions in two of their books.[41] They put considerable stress on understanding the basis of family leisure using sociometric techniques. They, too, are inclined to see the woman's position enhanced by greater mechanisation of everyday life (social and family), more extensive use of children's institutions and spreading the burden of housework more equally within the family.

O.I. Shkaratan has investigated problems of working-class social structure. His research contains interesting data on the everyday life of industrial workers in several Soviet cities.[42] Particularly noteworthy are his interpretation and information on provision of housing, furniture and home equipment, per capita average family income, social relations and social mobility within the urban population. Unfortunately, he too does not look at everyday life comprehensively.

Time-budget studies have gained momentum in recent years. But in the great stream of literature there is still little devoted explicitly to using time-budgets for investigating everyday life;[43] of course, any description of the non-working time of workers, employees and engineering and technical personnel can be valuable for urban studies as well. Researchers into everyday life have the task of studying time-budgets as an important and viable method of making a thorough and comprehensive analysis of the everyday life of Soviet people. They must follow the example of economists who treat time-budget studies as an instrument for examining the conditions of extended reproduction, the allocation and training of manpower resources, intensity of labour, living standards and provision of services.[44] Even a brief look at the issues shows that economists have put time-budget data squarely at the service of their science.

The general range of literature we have described shows that urban studies still await extensive research, even though particular aspects have been studied in a reasonably sound way using Soviet workers as examples. That is why we thought it necessary to provide an overview of Soviet urban studies. Before moving on to empirical studies, let us look at some of the experience of urban studies in capitalist countries.

2. Foreign urban sociology.

While noting the efficacy of studying foreign experience, we must emphasise the need for a discriminating approach to many phenomena which, though outwardly similar, are essentially different within capitalist and socialist societies. As the situation stands today, our literature has either ignored or given no adequate evaluation of even the fundamental theoretical conclusions and notions of the city in foreign scholarship. We shall therefore try to summarise in the most compressed and schematic way the principal schools of contemporary social urban research undertaken within the framework of that sub-section of bourgeois science known as 'the sociology of town life' or 'urban sociology'. The main trends in urban sociology may best be understood if we look at them chronologically, from the early 1920's to the mid-1960's.

Interest in urban studies has long been widespread in foreign publications and shows no sign of diminishing. Literature on urban themes is not only noticeably increasing, in certain areas it is becoming more profound. Works on the most diverse aspects of town life are published annually in many countries, notably in the USA, Britain, France and West Germany. A number of universities and academic institutions specifically study particular areas of urban life: the USA has the School of International Population and Urban Research at the University of California, the New York Sociological School and the Political Science Academy at Columbia University; Britain has its Centre for Urban Studies, and France its Sociological Research Centre, set up in 1946 as a branch of the National Research Centre.*

Although the range of problems, research objectives and methods have much in common in the above-mentioned countries, there are, of course, differences attributable to each country's specific conditions. The international conferences convened in the first postwar decade recognised the common nature of the problems and paramount role of urbanisation in the modern world. The first conference was held at the University of Chicago in 1953 and was dedicated to the impact of urbanisation on economic and cultural change. Those present included historians, sociologists, economists, ethnographers and geographers. Discussion was particularly lively on such issues as industrialisation in non-industrial countries, the evolution of towns in economically-advanced areas, the cultural role of cities, and spatial and economic factors in urban society.[45]

Scholars from four countries — USA, Britain, France and Denmark — took part in the second conference, held in 1954 at Columbia University in New York. They studied an even wider range of topics — in the realm of history, jurisprudence, sociology, archeology, the arts, theology, political science, engineering, architecture, geography, town planning, housing and municipal services. Most problems discussed at the conferences were concerned with the impact of large cities on specific institutions, the behaviour and views of the modern town-dweller.[46]

International conferences, symposiums and seminars on urban problems have also been convened under United Nations auspices.[47] They are normally associated with urbanisation problems in certain continents or areas of the world. A seminar was held, for example, in Bangkok in 1956 which mainly concerned itself with comprehensive urban development and the resultant social and economic factors affecting people's lives in Asia.[48]

Apart from international urban studies, it is worth mentioning the project, inaugurated at the University of Columbia in 1951 and subsequently transferred to the University of California, for compiling an Urban Resources Index on all the world's cities with a population in excess of 100,000. The Index is designed for research use and contains both historical data and current information on cities in different economic and cultural areas. Ultimately, it is intended to produce reasonably accurate and systematic comparisons, particularly on cultural standards, for studying the complex and variegated urbanisation processes.

---

* The Russian names have no literal American, British or French equivalent; it is assumed that these are the institutions to which they refer. [*JR*].

A. Boskoff summed up the problems being studied by bourgeois urban sociologists in the Preface to his book *The Sociology of Urban Regions*: "Sociologists are intensely interested in urban life and its extension for several reasons . . . Marriage and family problems, child rearing, crime, delinquency, migration, race relations, old age, mental health, social class, religion, education, and public opinion trends are just a few of the crucial problems that are found in, or derive from, an urbanised way of life."[49]

In their article "Urbanism and Social Structure", published in the book *Community Structure and Analysis*, Greer and Kube wrote that the historical development of sociology was closely bound up with the development of the town; the multitude of theoretical problems of concern to sociology were caused by forces which big cities create.[50] Greer developed these ideas further in a later book.[51]

In the opinion of the American historian and sociologist Kingsley Davis, the intent study of urban problems by bourgeois scholars has the following reasons. First, as distinct from such social institutions as the family, religion and language, towns are a relatively recent phenomenon in human history. Secondly, revolutionary changes in way of life and social structure are inherent in urbanisation as it emerges and develops. Thirdly, as they arise, towns become focal centres in relation to surrounding rural areas. And, fourthly, the rate of urbanisation is accelerating, so engendering fresh problems .[52]

Davis's argument is far from complete. He says nothing, for example, about the tendency for the urban share of the population to rise; he makes only muted reference to the growing scale of urbanisation. That is because, while the peasants are diminishing in all advanced capitalist countries, the working class, urban petty bourgeoisie, intellectuals and employees are expanding rapidly. The special attention that bourgeois scholars pay to various aspects of urban life may be attributed mainly to the fact that it is precisely in the towns, where most of the proletariat is concentrated, that the basic contradictions of contemporary capitalism, social and racial conflicts, are most acutely and painfully felt. Bourgeois researchers into urban problems, therefore, try to explain the chronic problems, to find ways of resolving old issues in the new situation and, last but by no means least, to defend or at least to conceal the class antagonisms and the incurable ills of capitalist cities.

The social problems immanent in capitalist towns coincide with the problems of class struggle which occupy a central place in the ideological life of contemporary capitalism. Moreover, many contentious ideological issues directly relate to changes in the working class and, above all, in its internal social structure, in cultural standards and the satisfaction of material needs. Acute social conflicts are producing many exculpatory theories, such as the 'deproletarisation' of society, the declining role of the working class in social affairs, its 'integration' within the capitalist system, etc.

Indeed, qualitative changes in economic progress certainly are occurring in the capitalist states in line with the scientific and technological revolution. They are causing a drastic change in the entire sphere of social relations, but they are not altering the nature of class and social relations in the capitalist town. Such towns are having their bourgeois-democratic basis eroded and replaced by a rigid stratification of relations expressed in a narrowing of the apex of the social pyramid and a widening and proletarisation of its base. This in turn exacerbates the social contrasts, makes the class and social conflicts of capitalist society even more strained; and that is bound to be reflected in the ideological conceptions of bourgeois science, including urban sociology.

Urban studies have a long history. To trace their development, we must start with American urban sociology which, in a certain sense, may be regarded as the 'classical' school with its own traditions and logic. At the same time, we cannot ignore results obtained elsewhere in the capitalist world; nor should any school be taken as a stereotype of urban sociology in general.

* * * * *

Urban sociology has long been recognised in the USA as an independent discipline, although rural sociology had become a specialised field somewhat earlier. In 1916, the annual meeting of the American Sociological Society had been devoted to 'rural sociology' and only in 1925 did it discuss the problems of 'urban sociology', the materials of which came out a year later.[53]

During the 1920's and in the early 1930's, which saw considerable expansion of empirical research in sociology, three scholars from the University of Chicago — Robert Park, Ernest Burgess and Roderick McKenzie — made a notable contribution to urban sociology and are considered to be the fathers of the ecological (or Chicago) school.[54] Their joint work, made up of essays they had written earlier, gives an idea of the substance and viewpoints of social ecology which was to become widely popular in Europe, too, during the 1930's, but under the title of 'social morphology'.[55]

The school was idealist in its theoretical orientation, in so far as it examined social urban problems on the premise of economic competition for urban space and the economic domination of big cities. In their attempt to locate the social forces of change in the racial and culturally-heterogeneous milieux of the city, proponents of the theory concentrated their efforts primarily on explaining the effect of competition on social advancement in local organisations. The research of the social ecologists is replete with fascinating observations of typical American phenomena (life of immigrants, juvenile delinquency, slums). They recognised the importance of cultural and even of psychological factors in urban life, yet they were incapable of defining their place in general theory. An eclectical mixture of the two schools of bourgeois science — social Darwinism and classical economism, which had been popular in the last century — underlies the theoretical concepts of Park, Burgess and the rest.

Social problems of city life found their expression in the 1920's not only in the works of the Chicago school. In 1929, the Lynds published the results of a study that spanned a long period (from 1880);[56] they defined their aim as presenting "a dynamic, functional study of the contemporary life of this specific

American community in the light of trends of changing behaviour observable in it during the last thirty-five years."[57] The research was based on a particular town which was given the name Middletown to mark its typical features as an average American town with a population of no more than 50,000 people.

Middletown had enormous success at the time; it ran into several editions and had a special seminar at Vienna University devoted to it. It served as the pattern on which analogous works are based even today. The Lynds took an institutional approach, carrying out widespread research into the urban community and especially the bureaucratic organisation and social structure of an average American town. Their methodological aims are characteristic of bourgeois sociology: they proceed from exculpative bourgeois conceptions, glossing over the acute contradictions between the working class and the capitalists.

Louis Wirth and Robert Redfield also had a considerable influence on the development of American urban sociology.[58] They made city life (its size, density, heterogeneity, etc.) the point of departure for their research, believing that urbanism was a way of life shaped by secularisation, secondary group relations, voluntary organisations, increasing role specialisation and barely perceptible social norms. Even a simple enumeration of such methodological premises shows that Wirth and Redfield picture the city as an ill-defined concrete social organism with barely distinguishable relationships. Nonetheless, their approach to the city as a major factor of development does have its attributes. The weakness of their theoretical views lies in the thematic incompleteness of urban sociology and, particularly, in the fact that although American urban sociology recognised (with some reservations) urban and rural communities as two parts of a large entity, it did not provide any explanation of exactly how to conduct research into these interconnected categories. Furthermore, social analysis based on the familiar rural-urban dichotomy has never been applied fully to either rural or urban sociology.

The 1940's and 1950's saw heightened interest in the various aspects of urban life, leading to further elaboration of urban ecology and demography,[59] the study of social organisation[60] and urban psychology.[61] The principal failing of these numerous works is that, in place of a searching analysis, they are dominated by idealist and statistical psycho-analysis. One may seek in vain for a historical analysis of facts related to the alignment and contention of class forces within the capitalist town. Facets of town life began to be reflected in the literature in this period: neighbourhood relations,[62] social effects of housing conditions,[63] 'moral' integration[64] and, particularly, race and ethnic relations.[65] Additionally, research into the urban impact on personality gained wide popularity. From a methodological standpoint, the works were speculative or, at best, hypothetical — even on the admission of bourgeois writers.[66] In fact, they show a clearly-expressed vindicative tendency designed to uphold the class interests of the bourgeoisie.

The wide sweep of urban sociological research naturally caused American urban sociologists to look again at the theoretical propositions of urban demography and ecology, and at the social organisation of cities. If we examine them critically, however, we see that, first, none of their premises were founded on a comparative approach to urban studies; secondly, certain universal formulations were unsuitable for empirical research; and, thirdly, the concepts of society applied to social organisation theory did not properly conform to the conceptions developed in the ecological school.

New views and ideas appeared in the 1960's. Many specialists had become dissatisfied with the tendency to study only individual segments of the social and economic structure of towns. They wished to study the town as an integral whole so as to use it as a laboratory for testing their theories and hypotheses. It became evident that any proper analysis of urbanisation problems required elucidation and definition of several key categories; urbanisation, the town, urban community, ecology, etc. In the interminable discussions on the question, there was little agreement.

Today, an abundance of schools still flourishes. Some stress external conditions and social structure as determinants of urban development; others prefer cultural values and political power. Meanwhile, even within the schools there is no concerted opinion on theoretical and methodological orientation.

The last decade or so has witnessed attempts to create a general theory of urban studies or, at least, to summarise existing theories. This mirrors the overall state of bourgeois sociology in which many sociologists realise the need for a general sociological theory. The functionalist school, with its dominant position in urban sociology, has been most active in theory-construction. Gideon Sjoberg,[67] for example, has written several works applying a structural-functionalist approach to the problem of synthesis or, in his own language "to understand and predict, by whatever theoretical or methodological tools are available, the social and ecological structure of cities or the actions of their ingabitants."[68] Despite the lack of success, one cannot deny his undoubted contribution to the study of social structure in American cities by combining theoretical and methodological tools in a single research-work.

No fewer than ten urban sociology schools currently vie for influence in American bourgeois society. We briefly mention the major ones below.

The urbanisation school, whose theoretical principles go back to Wirth and Redfield, is one of the most influential today. Sociological research recently conducted in the USA and elsewhere has exposed the weak points of its theoretical orientation.[69] O. Lewis, for example, has demonstrated that the urbanisation process in Mexico is not accompanied by the steady erosion of existing social and moral traditions.[70] The picture is similar in African towns where traditions are stubbornly holding their ground despite the strong influences of urbanism.[71]

Nevertheless, the views of Wirth and Redfield have remained quite strong both in urban sociology and in other, mixed areas, particularly in history which accords some importance to 'loss of identity' and 'alienation' in contemporary society.[72] Basing themselves on the traditional tenets of the urbanisation school, a group of American scholars have used a demographic foundation for their urban studies.[73]

Essentially, they put great store by measurement and use demographic data to encompass a wide range of phenomena whose study gives them a certain advantage in comprehending the nature of urban social organisation. This approach however, does not yet have a clear-cut theoretical orientation. In some instances, it is quite unclear whether urbanisation is defined in terms of size or whether size is seen as an index defining the concept 'town'. Neither approach elicits any objections, but no single analytical scheme is sufficient: size cannot be taken as the only criterion of a town. This approach therefore has a very narrow theoretical basis, is restricted in its application and grossly distorts reality.

A school based on the ecological complex still enjoys popularity in the USA. Essentially, it is an updated version of the old ecological approach free of certain social-Darwinist propositions. Its leading proponents are J.P. Gibbs, W.T. Martin, O.D. Duncan and L.F. Schnore. Their formative notions are strongly influenced by McKenzie, A.H. Hawley and Emile Durkheim (notably his ideas on division of labour). The leading lights of this school tend to be at loggerheads; this is apparent more on methodological than theoretical questions. J.P. Gibbs and W.T. Martin subscribe to the 'ecological complex' approach, using the inductive method. Duncan and Schnore tend to stress the 'means of subsistence' concept, using the so-called non-inductive approach. Let us take a closer look at these notions.

Duncan and Schnore include the environment, population, social organisation and technology among the determining elements in the ecological complex.[74] Evidently, these factors correlate functionally; changes in one lead to changes in the others. To illustrate their conclusions they adduce numerous data, largely collected from current census tracts; this facilitates measurement of the processes.

The work of Duncan and Schnore has serious shortcomings. In the first place, they are unable to explain the theoretical precepts by which their empirical research may be interpreted. Their device of identifying such concepts as 'social organisation' and 'division of labour' is particularly confusing. Moreover, they are wrong to assume that their four basic variables (environment, population, social organisation and technology) are of the same value. Evidently, they confuse social and physical-geographic factors. The second objection is that they err in regard to cultural values: they assert that they are either individual or reducing by nature. Furthermore, they tend to see cultural values in isolation from their basic theoretical model.

Gibbs and Martin focus attention on the means of subsistence. In *Urbanisation, Technology and the Division of Labour*,[75] they put forward the following four propositions:

(i) the extent of urbanisation in society changes directly in relation to the division of labour;

(ii) the division of labour in society changes directly with the distribution of consumer goods;

(iii) the extent of urbanisation in society changes directly in relation to technological development;

(iv) technological development in society changes directly in relation to distribution of consumer goods.

Using the ecological approach, Gibbs and Martin attempt to obtain as much information as possible, trying to gather it all into an organic whole. Yet their theoretical premises prove unsound the moment they apply cultural values to their basic propositions enumerated above. They base themselves on the false premise that cultural values have no connection with material production. Thus, they, too, have created an alternative approach to explaining urban activity.

Sjoberg belongs to the economic school of urban sociology.[76] He asserts that some of its members subscribe to Marxist ideas in classifying the town according to socio-economic formations and studying them historically. This method is, in fact, the one used by Soviet sociologists. Yet, in his article, Sjoberg is unable to name a single Western work on urban problems which had consistently applied a Marxist approach. He refers only to such writers as Eshref Shevsky and Wendell Bell[77] who form a special sub-group within the economic school. Their work gained renown exclusively by its methodology, classifying economic activity into "primary, secondary and tertiary types" which are, in turn, associated with different forms of urban economic and social structure.

It is exceedingly difficult to understand the real theoretical value of this approach because few works of any specific worth are available. Existing publications do show that no members of this sub-group of the economic school can be considered Marxist. Suffice it to say that the group includes people like S. Greer who ignores the influence of wide social structure on the life of local urban communities.[78]

Another group worthy of note is the natural environmental school. Although its influence in urban sociology is slight, it does have a fairly extensive readership. The historian and sociologist Lewis Mumford is its most prominent representative; he is known more as a moralist than a scholar, advocating very forthright views.[79]

Now and again Mumford mentions the forces of production of the modern city, but he focuses attention on the natural environment. He is perturbed by the 'danger' of rapid technical progress, the 'perniciousness' of technological progress. In his opinion, the town and its denizens should harmonise with the world of nature in order to function effectively. Given the causal nature of the natural environment, man should coordinate the forces of production and social organisation with the environment. Mumford believes the decisive problem facing modern society to be the lack of conformity between nature and the human culture being created in cities. In *The City in History*, he idealises the city of Athens in Ancient Greece, a model for present-day cities.

Mumford's utopian moralism and idealist views are clearly in evidence. The task confronting modern cities is not to adapt to the natural environment but to master nature and put it at the service of mankind. Yet we cannot agree with

Sjoberg's criticism of Mumford because he himself takes up a biological posture, pitting human beings abstractly against one another — while saying nothing about the class struggle between workers and capitalists.

We can only approach the question of the relationship between scientific progress and the natural environment by using historical materialist methods. If sociologists like Mumford had used that approach, they would be fighting for the meaningful liberation of man within capitalist society rather than throwing up abstract slogans.

Several influential schools started up in the USA in the early 1960's: notably the technological, cultural values and political power schools. While deliberating on the theoretical meaning of urban sociology back in 1959, Sjoberg had described them merely as orientations rather than schools in their own right.[80] In subsequent works, however, he elevated them to the status of schools.[81] Given the paucity of material it is hard to judge whether these approaches can be classed as fully-fledged schools in urban sociology or whether they represent trends of the above-mentioned urbanisation school. They certainly have become specialised areas and therefore merit at least some attention.

Of all the specialities, one of the most popular in urban studies today is that based on technology. Its proponents ascribe major significance to industrialisation as a mode of production; W.F. Ogburn may be cited as one of its foremost advocates. The empirical research which the school produces is of undoubted benefit when it emphasises **technical** development and its impact upon temporal and spacial aspects of the existence of towns. But certain propositions are highly debatable. Ogburn, for example, postulates that local transport affects the location of towndwellers, offices and residential blocks.[82]

The use of technology as a prime factor in urban studies necessitates careful consideration of the extent of industrialisation in countries at differing levels of industrial development. Research by a number of sociologists has shown, for example, that 'ideal models' established on American material are far from universally applicable in classifying data obtained in other cities of the world.

The theoretical orientation on technology as a prime factor in urban development may facilitate an understanding of urban social structure and the construction of models of different aspects of urban life. Yet the technological school has still to elucidate many concepts; hence the incomplete nature of its theoretical premises. It often uses technology in a very narrow sense, as in the case of several of Ogburn's views, or, on the contrary, it makes extreme generalisations which only hamper analysis.[83] Even though the theoretical parameters of the technological school have not yet been drawn with any finality, the unsoundness of the theory is generally apparent since it regards the city from the technological viewpoint alone and utterly fails to explain how changes in technology relate to social change and the repercussions this has on the character of urban life.

The methodological basis of the environmental school and the technological approach therefore expose the roots of bourgeois ideology. On the one hand, it appears in the form of technocracy, resting on structuralism and neo-positivism and, on the other, it appears in the guise of moral idealism — *i.e.*, subjectivism and existentialism.

Adherents of the 'cultural values' school select 'values' as their key determinant for studying the metropolis and for explaining the prevailing economic and social structure. Max Weber proposed just such an approach, believing the values of socio-cultural systems to be the principal factor of urban development, and social structure an element derived from it.[84] W. Firey, R.E. Dickinson[85] and W.L. Kolb[86] have all taken the theory further. Kolb, for example, has maintained that cultural values are the essential basis that explain urban ecological and social organisation. Cultural values exert decisive influence on the size of the town, population density and heterogenity. Clearly, this is, in effect, reiterating the factors mentioned by Wirth.

Nobody can ignore the important effect of cultural values on many features of urban life; it would be a gross mistake to underestimate them. But it is equally wrong to reduce cultural values to ideal classifications. They *may* serve as an essential criterion for comprehending many features of urban life as long as the researcher employs a correct methodology, consistently observes the principle of historicism. Cultural values should be seen in their relationship with urban economic and social structure. To separate culture from technological progress, as bourgeois scholars do, invariably invalidates material and impoverishes spiritual culture.

Finally, let us say a few words about the 'social power' school whose basic propositions were first formulated back in the 1950's.[87] Briefly, it highlights the excessive growth in social power. But it examines the effects of this quite out of the context of any urban social organisation at national or international level. In fact, this approach exceeds the bounds of urban sociology and bears an expressly political hue. To our minds, this approach belongs more to political sociology than urban sociology.

Behind all the current schools in contemporary American bourgeois urban sociology lies a certain feature of life that is looked at metaphysically, made into an absolute. This distorts any real understanding both of this feature itself and of urban life generally. It is not hard to discern that the schools of American bourgeois sociology are based on the theory of factors and reject the key principle of a materialist understanding of history — the decisive role played by the mode of production of material benefits in social development. Moreover, they put many factors on the same level: the economy, politics, culture, etc. To confuse fundamental and derivative social phenomena naturally leads to subjectivism and anarchy in evaluating social life.

* * * * * * * * * * * *

The multiple problems of urban life have received fairly intensive treatment in other capitalist states. In Europe, sociologists, historians, economists and geographers have focused attention largely on broad issues of urban sociology. A group of French researchers, for example, studied the 'social ethnography' of Paris[88] and one of its suburbs.[89] They described and analysed those aspects of urban life which come under the rubric of social ecology — *i.e.*, the relationship between the metropolitan area and economic, social, demographic and cultural phenomena.

The evolution of urban sociology in West Germany has been quite unique. Empirical studies connected with town planning and construction have gained wide popularity.[90] In *Die moderne Grossstadt*,[91] H.P. Bahrdt touches upon all manner of issues concerned with the history of urbanism, the family, public and private sectors, but he does dwell at some length on the social impact of town-planning methods. In his opinion, sociologists should have as much say in town planning as architects, construction-engineers and economists. The particular interest displayed by West German scholars in town planning stems mainly from the postwar reconstruction of German towns.

A.C. Hofmann and D. Kersten air the vital issue of a woman's double burden: in the home and in the factory. In their book *Frauen zwischen Familie und Fabrik*,[92] they employ a questionnaire-method to evince information on employment and the reasons why women go out to work. The questions cover husbands, family income, state of health and opportunities for giving up work. The authors conclude that the urban family in which a woman works needs assistance from the state and public organisations.

British publications, too, give full value to problems of urban life and contain a wealth of information about life in the city. While some issues are tackled in a theoretical way,[93] others tend to be more empirical.[94]

The book by F. Zweig,[95] for example, is of particular interest from the viewpoint of the factual material presented. He goes into some detail in describing aspects of an English worker's life such as: material living standards, family relations, dependence of domestic life on working conditions, the cultural outlook of the worker and his family, forms of leisure, religious denomination, etc. He gives a fairly full description of an English worker's life and work. The ideological ideas behind the book, based on the alleged growing similarity of the living standards of workers and of the so-called middle classes, are fallacious, being permeated with the ill-conceived notion of the disappearance of classes. They rest on the shaky foundation of an unscientific interpretation of the facts.

M. Young and P. Willmott in their *Family and Kinship in East London*,[96] say that, while ethnographers had described the system of kinship in primitive societies, they were actually the first sociologists to attempt to study kinship relations in an industrial society. The work was based on the resettlement of workers from a central urban area to one of London's new suburbs. In their research, the authors established that many people residing in the new estate complained they had been cut off from relatives remaining in the old area. Their conclusions point to the importance of kinship relations in an urbanised society, especially between a mother and her married daughter. Town councils and planners ought, therefore, to reckon with this.

Sociological research into town life has recently come alive in Japan.[97] Japanese urban studies are attracting the attention not only of Japanese sociologists, but of Europeans as well — like R.P. Dore.[98]

It remains to note that most of the work on urbanisation published in Europe and elsewhere owes much to American experience.

* * * * * * * * * * * * * *

Our brief survey of foreign urban studies enables us to draw some general conclusions. At the present time, as in the past, American bourgeois urban sociology is probably the most ill-defined area of all scientific research. If they exist at all, its boundaries are exceedingly indefinite. Some people even believe that urban sociology does not constitute a substantive outlook with a clearly formulated base. Contemporary bourgeois American urban sociology is, in fact, deeply entangled with other social sciences.

The methodological principles underlying urban sociological theory may be summed up as follows:

(a) They take a one-sided approach to towns;

(b) Towns are often examined without adequate consideration for the historically-formed economic system in which they exist;

(c) They spurn a genuinely scientific classification of social distinctions among towndwellers;

(d) Urban society is divided, in a purely mechanical way, into social, technological, cultural and other processes.

The various schools of contemporary bourgeois urban sociology contain a political hotch-potch of bourgeois views and try to reinforce them theoretically. and methodologically.

Any critical review of the work of bourgeois writers on urban social research would be incomplete if we did not mention the rational features. The greatest value of such work is that it does shed light on a whole number of important and interesting problems — even though it may not resolve them correctly by virtue of its fallacious theoretical orientation.

Also laudible are the rich factual and the vivid descriptions of many features of town life. That applies, in particular, to description and social analysis of slums which exist in every large American city where adverse social phenomena are most obviously manifest: poverty, destitution and the most diverse forms of social disorganisation — *i.e.*, social pathology of the individual and of groups. Slums are an incurable 'ulcer' of contemporary America.[99]

American urban sociologists have had considerable success in methods and research technique. To avoid unnecessary esoteric terminology, let us indicate only that, besides observations, interviews, questionnaires, study of documents and statistical processing, urban social research also makes wide use of such procedures as segregation indices, multiple repression coefficients and convariance analysis. It also has extensive recourse to mathematics and statistics, modern calculating and electronic techniques, which enable it more precisely to analyse multi-factor social phenomena. Yet, at the same time, it is surprising that it should lack a system of interrelated concepts, categories and terms reflecting important population processes in the capitalist city.

Nobody can deny the importance to the social sciences of quantitative methods when studying social processes. In their works, Marx and Lenin certainly regarded statistics very highly. Objective and subjective facts may be formalised, in most cases, and this broadens the scope for using in analysis various modes of quantification — *i.e.* quantitative expression of qualitative factors.

A situation has, however, developed in American urban sociology (and equally in other areas of sociology) where the lag in theory has inevitably led to an absolute concentration on statistical, methodological and technical devices. Such research techniques produce an obsession with purely quantitative methods, thus causing sociologists to study literally any single phenomenon restricted in time and space, which is utterly divorced from a circumspect investigation of social development as an integral whole. We recall Lenin's maxim that "facts are not only 'stubborn things' if you take them *as a whole*, in their *relationship* with one another; they are also invariably conclusive things. In fact, if you take them out of their entirety . . . then they are merely playthings or something worse."[100]

The greatest results in developing premises for a branch of knowledge like urban sociology can only be attained through profound historical experience and current practice. Most bourgeois scholars rely solely on abstract-quantitative methods and abstract-logical schemes and are, therefore, incapable of revealing — even less, objectively judging — the qualitatively unique nature of the processes immanent in modern urban society. Marxist theory alone can provide a correct understanding; the quantitative method of studying complex social phenomena of modern life may be useful only in conjunction with qualitative general conclusions. It is not all that rare today to see some bourgeois scholars forced to face up to Marxist theory and to employ certain of its propositions in a distorted form. Moreover, intellectual integrity is compelling some of them to adopt Marxist attitudes and this, perhaps, is making them our allies, irrespective of their consciousness.

Chapter 3

Soviet Urban Research

We rely in this work on state statistical data and material collected largely by our own social surveys. This chapter and the second paragraph of Chapter 4 are based on sociological research at Leningrad engineering plants.

The first survey, covering a wide range of social issues, was made by the Socio-Economic Problems Laboratory of the Leningrad Mechanics Institute. Researchers used an 'Interview Questionnaire' containing 54 questions relating to the work, cultural standards and leisure of Leningrad engineering workers. We have concentrated on information on living standards, cultural values, socio-political outlook, the family life of the worker and his family, household inventory and so on.

A two-stage district sample survey covering some 3,500 persons was used in selecting units for observation. Testing of the material gathered in 1965 by sample aggregation showed its adequacy for general aggregation on such key indices as wages, age, qualifications and general work record.

Processing of the information, carried out in three stages on the BESM—2M and the Minsk-2 computers, was completed in June, 1966. The author took part at the final stage of the investigation when a final analysis was made.[1]

In 1970, the Joint Institute Sociological Laboratory of the Concrete Social Research Institute of the USSR Academy of Sciences and the N.A. Voznesensky Leningrad Economic Finance Institute carried out a follow-up survey at the same Leningrad engineering works using analogous methods, programme and sampling scheme. The information obtained from these two pieces of research enable us to make a comparative analysis on a reliable factological basis.

We also utilised material collected in 1967 by the Joint Institute Sociological Laboratory of the Ethnographic Institute of the USSR Academy of Sciences and the N.A. Voznesenky Leningrad Economic Finance Institute in Kazan, capital of the Tatar Autonomous Soviet Socialist Republic and in two other Tatar towns — Almetyevsk and Menzelinsk. This research is of particular interest because the three towns differ in size and in the intensity of social processes taking place in them. We were able to compare a large industrial city (Kazan), a medium town with an oil-extractive industry (Almetyevsk) and a small town with a poorly-developed industry (Menzelinsk)*. Additionally, the Tatar Autonomous Republic is a reasonably average area in the USSR in major economic and social indices. And since the population of the three towns consists mainly of two national groups — Russians and Tatars, we were able to take ethnic factors into consideration.[2]

---

* In 1970, Kazan had a population of 870,000 and Almetyevsk 87,000 (see *Narodnoye Khozyaistvo SSSR, 1922-1972 gg.*, Moscow, 1972, pp. 20, 22). Menzelinsk had a population of some 15,000 (see *Bol'shaya sovetskaya entsiklopediya*, Moscow, 1974, Vol. 16, p. 212).

As in the previous research, information was collected by questionnaires, this time covering as many as 7,230 persons.³ The material collected from this sample survey was submitted to rigorous statistical and mathematical processing to test its representativeness. We are satisfied that the data obtained after computer processing was fully representative.

The author participated in all stages of gathering information, processing and analysis in the latter two surveys.

We use here a classification of industrial workers by occupational grade suggested by O.I. Shkaratan. Of course, his grades are not immutable or final; even less do they embrace the entire town population. But they are convenient for analysing the everyday life of different categories of working people: manual workers, engineering and technical personnel and employees — *i.e.*, the principal social strata of the Soviet urban population.* Problems of everyday life may be dealt with in different ways. In this book we take a basically sociological approach which enables us to discern the similarities and the dissimilarities in material and cultural satisfaction of people from different occupational groups and, thereby, to understand the major features of their everyday life.

1. Standard of living as an indicator of material life

The dynamics of change in public welfare reflect living standards — *i.e.*, the amount and nature of consumption of material and cultural benefits and the degree of satisfaction of material and cultural requirements. It would follow that such an intricate socio-economic category as welfare may only be distinguished by aggregated indicators. For example, the conditions of material life are most fully apparent when family income is estimated with account both for real earnings *and* for public funds, which affect living standards in socialist society. In Soviet experience, state aid is a very appreciable addition to family income particularly for families whose per capital income is still low.

We normally judge the standard of living of an individual, class or social group by consumption of material benefits. We shall therefore be looking at some of the more salient aspects of material welfare among the urban population, relying on synthetic and specific indicators.

One of the most important general indicators of welfare is the size of real income: earnings plus public consumption funds. Consequently, we must first turn to figures on wages growth as the basic index of family income in different social urban groups.

---

* See editor's introductory notes.

Under socialism, the steady growth in income is a natural consequence of development of the socialist mode of production. A higher level of welfare results from several sources. First, it comes from the planned growth of the earnings of manual workers, engineering and technical personnel andemployees. Just prior to 1962, the government made a major overhaul of the earnings-structure in industry, construction, transport, communications and farming. In 1964-65, it raised the wages of 20 million people engaged in direct service trades and, on January 1, 1965, it raised the minimum wage of workers and employees in all branches of the national economy which had not previously been increased. The resolution adopted jointly by the Party Central Committee and the USSR Council of Ministers on September 26, 1967 'On Measures Further to Improve Public Welfare'[4] is of particular importance because it resulted in an increase, from January 1, 1968, of the minimum earnings of workers and employees in all branches of the economy to 60 rubles a month and, of the minimum wage-scales and compulsory wage-rates for certain categories of worker, to 70 rubles a month. In the first half of 1968, it raised the wage-scales of machine-operators in the engineering and metal-working industries by an average of fifteen per cent throughout the economy. By a decree of the Presidium of the USSR Supreme Soviet 'On Reducing Taxation on Earnings of Workers and Employees'[5], the government cut income tax rates by an average of 25 per cent from January 1, 1968 on bachelors, single and small-family workers and employees earning between 61 and 80 rubles a month from their main workplace. Another measure was to increase paid holidays to fifteen working days for those workers and employees who had previously had only twelve working days with pay. After 1969, it raised the incomes of medium-paid groups in construction, construction-repairs and the building materials industry.[6]

The Party plans to launch a wide-ranging social programme in the immediate future aimed at improving material welfare even more. The Ninth Five-Year Plan Directives of the 24th Party Congress envisages an increase in per capita income by approximately 30 per cent.[7] Average earnings of workers and employees are to rise by 20-22 per cent, with a further rise in minimum wages.[8]

In addition to the increases in earnings, incomes have also risen by virtue of higher productivity. Labour productivity in Soviet industry rose overall by seven per cent between 1969 and 1970, while average monthly earnings of those engaged in the national economy showed a four per cent rise.[9] The average monthly earnings of Soviet workers and employees in the national economy were 122 rubles in 1970.[10]

In the light of this general information, let us take a specific look at average monthly earnings of Leningrad engineering workers by different occupational grade (see Table I).

Let us at once note that these figures refer to the beginning of 1970. They are interesting in that the average monthly wages of manual workers do not fall below 106 rubles, while earnings of skilled workers (groups 3, 4 and 5) exceed those of skilled mental workers. It is rather interesting that the percentage of engineering workers earning between 61 and 90 rubles a month is not generally

Table I

Earnings of Leningrad Engineering Workers Related to Nature of Work, 1970

Groups by nature of work	Percentage of workers with average monthly earnings (rubles)										Total as a percentage	Average earnings (rubles)
	Up to 60	61-80	81-100	101-120	121-135	136-150	151-175	176-200	201-250	Over 250		
1. Unskilled physical labourers	1.6	21.0	19.2	25.0	17.2	12.8	1.6	1.1	0.5	-	100.0	106.0
2. Low-grade mental workers	-	31.8	43.8	17.0	2.6	2.8	1.4	0.6	-	-	100.0	90.0
3. Skilled workers (mainly physical) operating machinery	1.3	3.4	12.5	15.3	10.4	16.6	16.1	16.8	5.9	1.7	100.0	142.0
4. Skilled workers doing mainly manual physical work	1.2	3.8	11.4	13.2	12.1	20.1	18.3	13.3	6.1	0.4	100.0	140.0
5. Highly-skilled workers combining mental and physical jobs	-	2.5	10.7	14.5	10.7	23.8	18.9	12.3	6.6	-	100.0	142.0
6. Skilled mental workers	-	1.1	12.7	24.8	22.2	19.8	10.0	5.6	2.0	1.8	100.0	131.0
7. Skilled mental workers doing engineering and technical work (excluding economists, lawyers, etc.)	-	1.4	7.6	25.2	18.0	23.2	14.2	8.1	1.4	0.9	100.0	134.0
8. Highly-skilled workers engaged in scientific and technological work	0.9	2.8	8.4	24.3	14.6	16.8	21.5	8.9	0.9	0.9	100.0	133.0
9. Supervisors of small departments	-	0.4	-	6.6	7.8	22.8	23.6	20.2	13.2	5.4	100.0	168.0
10. Supervisors of large departments (from workshop superintendent upwards)	-	1.1	-	1.1	2.1	13.8	14.9	29.8	26.6	10.6	100.0	191.0

high, with the exception of unskilled physical labourers and low-grade mental workers, whose figures are 21 and 31.8 respectively. It is noteworthy that a substantial number of skilled workers take home a monthly income of over 150 rubles (40.5, 38.1 and 37.8 per cent in groups 3, 4 and 5 respectively).

Supervisors of departments (particularly workshop superintendents and higher grades) surpass all other occupational grades in earnings. The lowest paid are low-grade mental workers without a specialist education (90 rubles a month).

The earnings of Leningrad engineering workers rose steadily throughout the period 1965-70 from 113 to 134.5 rubles a month. The rise was especially marked for those doing mainly physical work — machine operators, fitters, etc. While unskilled and low-skill physical labourers without a specialist training earned 97.5 rubles in 1965, they were earning 106 rubles a month in 1970. Skilled workers doing mainly physical work operating machinery earned 142 rubles in 1970, as against 107.5 rubles a month in 1965, while skilled workers doing mainly manual physical work boosted their monthly earnings from 120 to 140 rubles over the period.

It is also interesting that the earnings of skilled mental workers rose less rapidly in the space of five years than did those of manual workers. For example, construction engineers earned an average of 127 rubles a month in 1965, and 133 rubles in 1970; economists, technologists, etc., had a salary rise from 109.8 to 131 rubles; supervisors of workshops, departments, etc., increased their earnings from 172.9 to 191 rubles a month over the period.

The picture would not be complete if we ignored the importance of additional earnings and garden allotments to Leningrad engineering workers.

The figures on additional earnings indicate that, first, the great bulk of the labour force have none at all, and secondly, if people do have any, they usually amount to less than 50 rubles a month. Among workers doing mainly skilled physical labour, additional earnings normally amount to no more than 30 rubles a month.

On the evidence of the 1965 survey, we may conclude that as the number of family members with an independent source of income increases, a certain pattern emerges in regard to possessing a country cottage, a garden allotment or home farm. As many as 90.2 per cent of Leningrad engineering worker-families with two members working had no home farm, garden allotment or personal cottage; the figure falls to 82.5 and 81.3 per cent for families with four and five regular wage-earners respectively. It is worth noting that home farms figure much less than country cottages and garden allotments, whose number increases in step with the number of independent wage-earners in a family. The proportion of cottages and garden allotments rises from 7.3 per cent for families with two wage-earners to 16.9 per cent for families with five regular wage-earners. On the whole, the significance of home farms, garden allotments and personal cottages in 1965 was not very great, in so far as 87.9 per cent of Leningrad engineering workers generally did without them.

None of these three items can be related to social origin. Thus, 88.0 per cent of the 'have-nots' were manual workers by origin, 88.1 per cent were collective farmers and 84.8 per cent were employees. This situation suggests that possession of a home farm, garden allotment or personal cottage depends more on material means, personal inclination and residential location (inside or outside city limits) than on social origin. Other factors would seem to operate as well, such as the influence of relatives and friends, whether the factory has a well-run collective gardening establishment, etc.

A follow-up survey in 1970 showed that 80.0 per cent of the Leningrad engineering workers did not have a home farm, garden allotment or country cottage. Of these, only a tiny number of families (between 1.5 and 4.5 per cent) had a home farm. The use of a garden or orchard allotment or a personal cottage was much more marked. A pronounced pattern emerges showing a diminishing share of home farms as occupational grade rises.

That is not so with garden allotments, orchards and country cottages, which increased by four-five per cent on average in the space of five years. Here, mental workers surpass physical labourers by a ratio of almost 2 : 1. In the forseeable future, we may expect an increase in these gardens and cottages because many families see in them not simply a means to satisfy material and cultural requirements, but a base for summer holidays, amateur gardening, etc. — *i.e.*, factors that auger well for personality -development.

Another noteworthy feature of the research is that, as with the surveys of the 1920's and 1930's, the lower-paid worker-family members in our sample were predominantly the second and third members of the family. These were largely women, young men and girls. Per capita family income would, therefore, be a more meaningful index of the level of material welfare, enabling us to group families by degree of material security. Of course, this type of grouping also has its drawbacks. Size of income depends on the size of the family, the number of wage-earners in the family and the amount of their earnings. There is here a number of statistically - verified patterns. Big families normally have a lower per capita income and small families have a relatively high average income per family-member.

Income grouping per family-member, as P.P. Maslov has rightly pointed out, may nonetheless help us to make certain analytical conclusions about overall living standards and income structure.[11] Table II shows average earnings per family-member among Leningrad engineering workers in 1970.

Per capita family income, amounting to an average of 75 rubles 27 kopecks, varies with occupation. Unskilled and skilled workers, mainly doing manual physical labour, have the lowest per capita income (73 rubles), except for low-grade mental workers who have an average per capita family income of 68 rubles 89 kopecks. Average earnings per family-member among all mental workers differ only slightly from workers mainly engaged in physical labour. The only exception are families of department supervisors (from workshop superintendents upwards) which have a per capita income of 82 rubles 60 kopecks. Of all the occupational grades listed, only a very small number of families (fewer than 5.0 per cent) have an average per capita income of less than 40 rubles a month.

If we compare the figures on average earnings per family-member among engineering workers in 1965 and 1970, we can see the changes that have occurred. Income per family-member increased more substantially among manual workers by comparison with mental workers. Thus, in 1965, per capita income in unskilled and low-skill worker-families was 60.8 rubles against 73.2 rubles in 1970. Skilled workers operating machinery and those engaged in mainly physical labour had an even greater increase over the five years. The families of these two groups of workers had a per capita income of 64.5 and 62.3 rubles a month in 1965, which rose to 76.9 and 73.4 rubles respectively in 1970.

The picture is somewhat different for mental workers. The families of technologists, economists, etc., were earning 67.2 rubles a month in 1965 per family-member, which increased to 75.3 rubles in 1970. The families of highly skilled workers engaged in scientific and technical work had an increase in per capita earnings over the same time-span only of 72.2 to 75.2 rubles. (Table II)

The per capita family-member earnings of workshop superintendents and above, however, rose from 71.1 in 1965 to 82.6 in 1970.

From all these figures we may draw the conclusion that the real earnings of Leningrad engineering workers are steadily increasing. They remain the major structural part of the family incomes of workers, engineering and technical personnel and employees and, therefore, serve as a key source for satisfying the various requirements of workers and their families. Furthermore, there is no excessive differential between the incomes of the different occupational groups; that undoubtedly contributes to the growing democratisation of Soviet society, to social mobility and the erosion of differences among the various social strata and groups.

Low-paid categories are still in evidence. This unresolved problem is certainly being attended to by our Party and government, which constantly show concern for raising minimum earnings. We should emphasise the point that present-day economic development does not yet permit us to raise the earnings of absolutely all categories of workers substantially above the subsistence wage.

The public funds, made up of contributions from state and public organisations, are of major importance in ensuring higher living standards. At the present time, gratuitous payments and benefits are obtainable in the form of social security, allowances, pensions, student grants, free medical care and education, kindergartens, sanatoria, rest homes, etc. "Distribution via public funds," as A.S. Kovalchuk rightly points out, "is intended somehow to make up and compensate for historically-conditioned and thereby inevitable *de facto* inequality existing in remuneration by work done. That, of course, has nothing in common with wage-levelling ... This is the special social role of the public funds under socialism, which help us to achieve greater equality in distributing material and cultural benefits."[12]

Table II

Average Per Capita Family Earnings Related to Occupational Group, 1970*

Groups by nature of work		Percentage of workers with gross monthly earnings per family member (rubles)							Total as a percentage	Average cash earnings per family-member (rubles)
	Up to 30	31-40	41-50	51-60	61-70	71-80	81-100	Over 100		
1. Unskilled physical labourers	2.1	4.8	6.8	13.8	15.9	16.8	24.4	15.4	100.0	73.27
2. Low-grade mental workers	1.1	4.7	12.8	17.1	17.2	17.9	20.6	8.6	100.0	68.89
3. Skilled workers (mainly physical) operating machinery	0.8	3.5	7.0	13.0	12.7	16.3	26.5	20.2	100.0	76.95
4. Skilled workers doing mainly manual physical work	0.8	4.0	9.2	14.5	15.9	16.3	23.0	16.3	100.0	73.40
5. Highly-skilled workers combining mental and physical jobs	3.3	2.5	4.1	12.3	15.6	18.8	25.4	18.0	100.0	75.45
6. Skilled mental workers	0.7	2.0	9.3	11.6	16.6	19.3	22.7	17.8	100.0	75.26
7. Skilled mental workers doing engineering and technical work (excluding economists, lawyers, etc.)	1.4	3.3	1.4	12.8	16.8	20.9	19.5	13.9	100.0	71.40
8. Highly-skilled workers engaged in scientific and technological work	0.9	1.4	6.5	9.9	23.8	16.3	26.3	14.9	100.0	75.23
9. Supervisors of small departments	0.3	3.1	5.4	11.0	16.7	14.0	24.8	24.7	100.0	78.21
10. Supervisors of large departments (from workshop superintendent upwards)	1.1	1.7	4.2	5.0	16.0	10.0	32.0	30.0	100.0	82.60

* Cash earnings per family-member are estimated after tax deductions and receipt of benefits, including permanent wages, pensions, grants, supplementary earnings and other family income.

It is particularly noteworthy that average earnings of Soviet industrial workers with the addition of payments from public funds amounted to 164 rubles in 1970 against 158 rubles in 1969.[13] Since state statistics show more than one member of the family working,[14] the average monthly earnings of urban families, with the addition to wages of other payments and benefits, amounted to 252 rubles in 1969.[15]

Consequently, supplementary payments and benefits play an important part in material and cultural welfare. It is by virtue of the indirect benefits that per capita income in the USSR increased by 1.3 times between 1965 and 1969, and more than ten-fold since 1940.[16] The 24th Party Congress Five-Year Plan Directives announced a 40 per cent increase in public consumption funds.[17]

So we see that real incomes are increasing, wages are rising and supplementary income from public funds is acquiring increasing significance. This means considerably more purchasing power for the urban population, as is patently clear from the figures on state and cooperative retail trade-turnover, including public catering. While the trade-turnover had risen by 435 per cent between 1940 and 1965, the increase was 601 per cent by 1969.[18]

Rising trade turnover shows a growing demand for and purchases of foodstuffs and clothing during the 1960's. This was encouraged by price-cuts on a number of commodities. The 1969 price index (1960 = 100) for selected consumer goods was as follows: 90.1 on woollen cloth, 78.6 silk cloth, 90.3 clothing and linen, 98.2 knitted fabrics, 89.2 stockings and socks and 98.3 haberdashery.[19] In March, 1971, further price cuts were made: between 19 and 30 per cent on TV sets, 16 per cent on washing machines, 19 per cent on motorcycles and 15 per cent on nylon raincoats, etc.[20]

The USSR is approaching scientifically-established norms and does not lag behind industrially-advanced capitalist states in consumption levels of a number of prime consumer goods (excluding foodstuffs).[21]

The Soviet population consumes an average of 3,000-3,200 calories every day.[22] This bears witness to the fact that the Soviet Union has completely resolved the food problem in regard to calory-intake per inhabitant; the scientifically established consumption norm now coincides with the number of calories consumed by each inhabitant. The task now is to improve the food-consumption structure.

Information in Table III was obtained from three Soviet towns and applies to the structure and quantity of food consumption in worker-families.[23] The picture has obviously changed out of all recognition since before the revolution. In consumption of such products as meat, milk, eggs, sugar and potatoes, the families of textile-workers in the three towns are now approaching scientifically established norms.[24]

Public catering establishments, whose turnover increases every year, are having a big effect on the quantitative and qualitative improvements in the food consumption of Soviet towndwellers.[25] The further expansion of public catering owes much to the resolution of the Party Central Committee and USSR Council of Ministers "On Measures for Promoting and Improving Public Catering."[26]

Table III

Food Consumption by Textile-Worker Families of Leningrad, Noginsk and Furmanov in 1968 and 1913

Foodstuff	Annual per capita average (kg.)		1968 as percent of 1913
	1913	1968	
Meat and fats (including poultry and natural bi-products)	22.2	66.4	294
Milk and dairy produce (estimated in milk	87.0	346.8	399
Eggs (number)	53.	225	421
Fish and fish products	14.5	20.6	142
Sugar	9.4	36.9	393
Potatoes	90.2	119.7	133
Vegetables and melons	41.0	71.9	175
Bread products (bread estimated in flour, flour, cereals, leguminous and macaroni products)	174.3	121.0	69

Material welfare very much depends on the way people are housed.* On the one hand, housing is a product of material production, while, on the other, it is a consumer commodity which is as crucial as food, footwear, and so on. Housing is vital to satisfaction of individual requirements, the inculcation of moral qualities and culture — *i.e.*, all aspects of everyday life. The housing situation strongly affects many features of social life in its many-sided manifestations: housing may encourage or hinder the development of the individual and social groups; it may encourage psychical equilibrium or be the cause of psychic disorders; it may have a good or bad effect on the formation of social relations. Housing also shapes many features of everyday life and the personal requirements of the urban population: housing conditions influence human reproduction, the harmonius development of the personality and, in the final analysis, give us a fairly clear picture of the cultural standards of towndwellers.

Soviet efforts in tackling the housing problem are generally known. Between 1966 and 1970 alone, we built a total of 518 million square metres of housing space and ameliorated the housing conditions of nearly 55 million people.[27]

---

* It should be borne in mind that, with the exception of people living in wooden houses — which are gradually being demolished, Soviet town-dwellers live in blocks of flats.

In the same period, getting on for 246,000 Leningrad families either moved into new homes or had their housing conditions improved.[28]

The survey of Leningrad engineering workers showing amount of housing space per family-member related to nature of work produced some rather interesting results. They show a marked levelling out in the distribution of accommodation. The mean size of living space fluctuates in the occupational grades from 6.4 to 8.8 square metres, thus giving an average of 7.0 square metres per person.

The Leningrad housing situation showed a marked improvement in all occupational groups between 1965 and 1970. Each family-member of unskilled and low-skill physical and mental workers lacking specialist training had an average of 6.1 square metres in 1965; this rose to 7.3 square metres in 1970. Living-space improvements, by 0.4 and 0.6 square metres, also occurred for skilled workers engaged mainly on machine-handling and those doing mainly manual physical labour. These categories of workers disposed of 6.4 and 6.8 square metres respectively per family-member in 1970.

The housing conditions of mental workers similarly improved. Thus, for skilled mental workers and highly-skilled scientific and technical personnel, the per capita family living-space rose from 6.8 and 6.7 to 7.5 and 7.8 square metres respectively. Families of supervisors increased their accommodation from 7.0 in 1965 to 8.8 square metres per person in 1970.

The average living space per family-member among Leningrad engineering workers increased by more than 1.5 square metres during the five years. The difference in living space between the various groups has diminished and is now no more than 2.2 square metres per family-member.

Data on amount of living accommodation per person are, without doubt, the basic index on housing conditions. To gain an even fuller picture, however, we need to look at material showing the extent of isolation of urban dwellers. Our assumption here is that an isolated dwelling considerably influences the formation of the foundation of everyday life and of the entire urban way of life.

Substantial changes occurred in this respect between 1965 and 1970. While 20.2 per cent of engineering workers had separate flats in 1965, 27.4 per cent occupied flats in 1970 with two or more rooms, and 8.8 per cent lived in single-room flats. We may note that in 1970 separate flats with two or more rooms went to 20.2 per cent of families of unskilled and low-skill physical and low-grade mental workers lacking specialist training, 21.4 per cent of skilled workers engaged mainly on machine-handling, 27.4 per cent of skilled workers engaged mainly on manual physical work, 31.3 per cent of engineering and technical personnel (technicians, economists, etc.), 34.1 per cent of highly-skilled scientific and technical personnel and 53.9 per cent of supervisors.[29]

It is certainly a good sign that fewer engineering workers are living in hostels (a fall from 7.8 in 1965 to 6.2 per cent in 1970).

Only 3.3 per cent of families living beyond the city boundaries, sometimes even at quite a distance, have their own homes. It would seem that urbanisation with all its consequences is engulfing vast areas and forming numerous settlements of country cottages and blocks of flats around cities. Leningrad in that respect is very typical.

The figures indicate the absence of any marked difference in degree of isolation of housing among mental and manual workers.

In studying living standards as an index of the material side of urban life, it is important to look at statistics that show the interrelationship between the basic features of everyday life and various social and demographic characteristics. We may illustrate this from the example of Kazan (see Table IV).

Table IV

Relationship Between Everyday Life Indices and Social and Demographic Characteristics of the Population of Kazan, 1967 (in Chuprov coefficients)*

	Wages	Per capita family earnings	Existence of home farm	Isolation of housing	Living space per family-member	Structure of household inventory
Occupational structure .	0.225	0.122	0.054	0.131	0.093	0.156
Education	0.160	0.122	0.050	0.130	0.094	0.165
Nationality	0.079	0.039	0.030	0.047	0.053	0.076
Age	0.161	0.094	0.060	0.124	0.088	0.084

* The Chuprov coefficient formula is:
$$T = \sqrt{\frac{x^2}{N \cdot S}},$$
where x^2 is the K. Pearson conformity criterion, N is the size of the statistical sample, S is the degree of freedom.

N.B. The Chuprov coefficient, by contrast with the Pearson criterion, may express the extent of the relationship between factors being measured quantitatively and those not being measured quantitatively, without any assumption about the form of their distribution.

Table IV shows that occupational structure and education have the most marked effect on everyday life. Age has less influence, although it is still noticeable. In the case of a home farm (or garden allotment), the figures show a virtual complete lack of any dependence of indices. It is evident that nationality has absolutely no effect on the factors that constitute the basis of urban everyday life.

The material side of everyday life, forming as it does the foundation for the whole intricate complex of urban life, is a vital element in our urban way of life and greatly stimulates the democratisation of Soviet society. Both these aspects of social life may be seen as a problem of the relationship between the social micro- and macro-system.

Material urban life is becoming increasingly uniform. Social and demographic factors have the most babearing on this process, national factors considerably less. The result is to consolidate and bring the socialist nationalities closer together. Although this national 'convergence' is a complicated process, it is manifestly taking place in the basic spheres of human endeavour, including everyday life.

In examining the welfare issue, we must also take another major factor into account, even though it does not leave its mark directly on living standards. That is the total absence of unemployment in the USSR and the resultant confidence of every worker in the future.

The material cited above testifies to the fact that we are meeting the growing material requirements of the Soviet urban population with increasing regularity; we are achieving this through a rapid growth and constant improvement in production. As Lenin once put it, production is being organised "to ensure the *complete* welfare and free *all-round* development of *all* members of society."[30]

2. *Cultural values and everyday life*

Contemporary social science conventionally uses the concept 'culture' in two senses. First, it has a wide meaning, covering the entire many-sided complex of society's material and cultural progress, continually developing within specific historical boundaries. Secondly, it has a narrow meaning, coinciding with that of 'spiritual culture', being confined to phenomena being formed in the process of human spiritual activity.[31] The functions of spiritual culture are variegated, giving some idea of culture both as a process of spiritual production and as ways and means of distributing and mastering already-created spiritual wealth — *i.e.*, as consumption of cultural values primarily in everyday life.

The specific meaning of culture as a creative process of spiritual value-formation, the distribution and mastery of spiritual values by society may only be understood in a Marxist way — *i.e.*, by examining the causal effect of socio-economic relations on the formation and character of the fundamentals of spiritual culture. This approach reveals the superstructural nature of spiritual culture as being determined by the basis of the given society and objectively reflecting social being. When people creatively master spiritual culture, it becomes part of their activity in all relations with one another (spiritual contacts, work, everyday life and social affairs).

The consumption of cultural values in Soviet towns is a complicated and still understudied problem from methodological and procedural standpoints. We look at only a few aspects of the consumption of cultural values as related to the cultural and political orientation of the urban population, drawing attention primarily to the growing similarity between the overall cultural standards of different grades of workers in Leningrad, Kazan, Almetyevsk and Menzelinsk.

To learn something of these questions we give brief information on the educational standards of manual workers and improvement in their vocational skills. We do this because, under socialism, the working class, being the leading social and political force, takes an active part in enjoying cultural achievements, on the one hand, and in forming a new type of culture, on the other. The working class should therefore be looked at both as a subject mastering scientific, technical, social and other values, and as an object shaping the basis of general human culture.

Modern production is constantly under the impact of scientific progress. It exerts a direct influence on the growth of both general and specialised education of workingmen. Economic development is nowadays unthinkable without mechanisation and automation which, in turn, demand an ever increasing number of skilled workers capable of understanding and operating the latest plant and equipment.

The growing complexity of production and the rising educational standards are resulting in more and more educated workers being able to turn their hand and brain to physical and mental work. This also indicates how rapidly we are now able to efface the essential differences between physical and mental labour.

Understandably, specialist technical knowledge can only be obtained with a high level of general education, a knowledge of the fundamentals of several exact and humanitarian sciences, and mastery of the achievements of spiritual culture. But it is no simple task to shape the foundation of spiritual life. The development of a scientific outlook among Soviet workingmen is a lengthy, continual and intricate process requiring enormous effort. That is why the Party, following Lenin's instructions, is guided in its day-to-day work by long-term plans that encompass all aspects of the spiritual life of the working class.

The vast work done by our Party and government in radically transforming and expanding education and in spreading cultural enlightenment led to major changes in the cultural outlook of modern workers. Even in 1929, for example, there were only 8.3 per cent illiterates among Leningrad iron and steel workers, while young industrial workers generally had at least a six-year education.[32] Particularly giant strides have been taken in recent years in raising the general educational standards of Leningrad workers. By 1969, for example, 59 per cent of Leningrad workers engaged mainly on physical labour had an incomplete secondary or a complete secondary education.*[33] This increase in educated workers is due to the rising proportion of secondary school-leavers in the composition of the working class. It is also indicative that thousands of workers are supplementing their education by attending factory or evening school. Leningrad had 46,900 persons in forms nine, ten or eleven of general secondary schools in the 1966-67 school year.[34] In addition, 67,900 were attending similar classes in schools for working youth and adult-education centres.[35]

* An incomplete secondary education is normally eight years of schooling; a complete secondary education is ten years.

Some 35,000 and 34,800 people matriculated from Leningrad secondary schools in 1968 and 1969 respectively.[36] Of the 500,000 persons attending general educational schools and schools for working youth in 1968, 81,000 were combining study with work. Despite these encouraging figures, it remains a fact that many workers make no effort to improve their general educational level.

The Leningrad survey shows that far more students are to be found in the skilled groups than in the unskilled. As many as 89.9 and 95.2 per cent of all unskilled workers were not studying in 1965 and 1970 respectively. The corresponding figures were 76.9 and 82.5 per cent for skilled workers doing manual physical labour. It should be noted that highly-skilled manual workers surpass all other manual grades in number of students at higher educational establishments, thus showing convergence in educational standards between these manual workers and those engaged in mental work.

The fact that a large number of workers is studying at higher educational establishments or on preparatory courses for entry into higher education shows that for many workers secondary education is not an end in itself, but a step towards further education in tekhnikums* or evening institutes. Leningrad colleges had 272,000 students in 1968; of these 146,000 were working.[37] In the same year, the tekhnikums and other secondary specialised schools in Leningrad and the Leningrad Region had 132,000 students, of whom 66,000 were combining work and study.[38] In 1968 and 1969 alone, some 124,000 specialists graduated from the city's higher and secondary specialised colleges.[39]

The fact that so many Soviet workers have the opportunity to obtain a higher or secondary technical education once again testifies to the immense advantages of the socialist over the capitalist system. Expenditure on education in the USSR is several times greater per head of population than it is in the advanced capitalist states; thus it is S113 in USSR, but only S35 in France, S32 in USA and S28 in West Germany annually.[40]

We cannot, of course, force all workers to study. But if we can understand the reasons that prevent workers from studying, we may be able to remove the major obstacles and map out ways to involve them more widely in general education. We provide below some figures on education obtained in 1970.

---

* Tekhnikums are technical schools (normally from age fifteen) with three or four year courses designed for intermediate technical personnel of all kinds — *e.g.*, nurses, primary school teachers, technicians, clerks.

Table V
Reasons Preventing Leningrad Engineering Workers from Studying, 1970 (%)

Groups by nature of work	Shift	Age	Home conditions, distance of home from work	Running the home, care of children	State of health, great fatigue from work	Work does not require much knowledge	Additional work	Big gap in studies	No desire	Other reasons	No reply
Unskilled physical workers	2.0	55.0	4.5	7.2	3.0	1.5	0.5	3.5	10.6	8.0	4.2
Skilled workers doing mainly physical work handling machinery	5.8	37.8	4.3	9.0	4.4	1.9	-	5.4	17.6	10.0	3.8
Skilled workers doing mainly manual physical labour	3.6	34.3	4.0	8.6	4.6	1.5	2.0	6.9	10.3	11.0	13.2
Highly-skilled workers combining mental and physical jobs	3.7	37.3	4.5	12.0	3.0	1.5	3.7	3.7	6.7	10.5	13.4

The largest number of workers not improving their education give age, followed by running the home and care of children, as their main reasons. The same reasons predominated in 1965 as well. Nevertheless, the five-year span saw a considerable reduction in persons giving unsatisfactory home conditions or remoteness from place of work as major obstacles to study. In 1965, as many as 13.5 per cent of unskilled physical labourers and 15.6 per cent of skilled workers doing mainly manual work gave this as their reason.

Other reasons given would appear to be less important than those already mentioned. We may note in passing that running the home and care of children fall mainly upon women, which naturally prevents many of them from continuing their education. All skilled groups show a high percentage of persons who do not study for reasons not included in the list. We may suppose that here lie reserves that could be tapped for drawing many more workers into general education.

It is beyond the brief of this book to examine the scope and structure of vocational training and the growth in apprenticeships which, along with general education, serve as a basic index of standards of spiritual culture. Nonetheless, it should be recorded that many new personnel are trained and many others improve their skills every year in Leningrad. An increasing number of skilled workers is being trained in Leningrad vocational schools, which also provide a general secondary education for their charges. Some 35,000 and 38,200 persons were trained through this channel in 1968 and 1969 respectively.[41] Obviously, the more we introduce up-to-date technology and techniques requiring all-round and wide-ranging technical knowledge, the more important become vocational schools and colleges able to supply the economy with such personnel.

As many as 340,000 people improved their qualifications or acquired new skills by indivdual study, class work or courses directly at work in Leningrad and the Leningrad Region.[42]

The wide scope of training and improvements in qualifications suggests that the gap between the general and specialist education of workers will steadily close as science and technology develop. Specialist education will not only be based on general education, it will increasingly coincide with it. The growing similarity of the different forms of general education and vocational training will have an immense influence on the whole process of improving the spiritual culture of the working class and removing the differences between occupational grades, particularly of manual workers and technical personnel.

Spiritual values are not confined to general education and vocational training. We agree with V.A. Yezhov that "in looking at education as the prime index of a worker's cultural development, we should not forget that a socialist cultural revolution requires attention to be paid to other factors which distinguish the worker's cultural make-up in Soviet society."[43] That point is just as valid for engineering and technical personnel and for employees.

A principal index of a person's spiritual culture is his cultural and political orientation. Many factors go to shape the cultural and political outlook of the

Table VI

Effect of Occupation on Cultural and Political Standards, 1970 (% given for number of people questioned according to each factor)

Factors determining cultural level	Read newspapers			Read political literature			Read (fiction) books				Possess their own books (library)						Go to the theatre		
Groups of engineering workers	regularly	Irregularly	not at all	regularly	Irregularly	not at all	1 book a week or more	1-2 books a month	less than 1 book a month	not at all	not at all	1-10 books	11-50 books	51-100 books	101-500 books	over 500 books	no less than once a month	a few times a year	never
Unskilled physical workers	55.5	28.9	15.6	12.9	23.4	63.7	20.4	32.8	21.3	25.5	26.9	21.9	26.9	15.6	3.2	5.6	22.6	40.5	36.9
Skilled workers doing mainly physical work handling machinery	75.2	20.6	4.2	20.9	34.5	44.6	37.1	42.8	12.4	7.7	16.2	23.9	37.1	13.2	7.6	2.0	33.7	50.9	15.4
Skilled workers doing mainly manual physical work	79.9	17.9	2.2	21.1	41.6	37.3	33.1	46.2	16.1	4.6	9.8	18.8	40.8	18.2	8.6	3.8	31.8	53.8	14.4
Highly-skilled workers combining mental and physical jobs	84.5	14.0	1.5	24.6	40.1	35.3	33.9	30.8	29.2	6.1	9.2	13.8	37.1	18.4	15.4	6.1	23.0	61.6	15.4
Highly-skilled scientific and technical personnel	71.9	26.7	1.4	16.1	56.2	27.7	28.5	46.9	23.9	0.7	3.6	6.6	21.6	27.6	33.3	7.3	27.4	66.7	5.9

diverse groups of towndwellers, particularly manual workers and technical personnel. They include a person's occupation, his level of skill, education, job-responsibility, earnings, demographic factors and, especially, age, sex and ethnic characteristics.

From Table VI we can see the effect of occupation on **attitudes** to cultural and political values.

With rising occupational status, interest in reading newspapers and books increases, as does the desire to have a home library. A fundamental distinction exists, in regard to reading newspapers, between unskilled physical labourers and all other groups. Moreover, we see that interest in newspapers among all other groups is more or less the same, except that it is slightly less for highly-skilled scientific and technical personnel.

There would appear to be no marked difference among groups in regard to theatre attendance. The only deviation is among workers combining mental and physical work and scientific and technical personnel who show a slight reduction in regular theatre attendance. This may be due to the fact that such persons improve their cultural standards via other mass communication channels.

A certain deviation from the general trend is the interest in political literature which diminishes somewhat with rise in qualifications. The percentage of highly-skilled scientific and technical personnel reading such literature falls to 16.1 — *i.e.*, lower than in all skilled groups. True, the percentage of irregular readers of political literature in this group is 56.2, and only 27.7 per cent read nothing political at all. Nonetheless, it would seem that the percentage of persons not reading political literature declines as qualifications rise.

If we compare figures for 1965 with those of 1970, we again have to face the unpalatable fact that 15.4 per cent of unskilled physical labourers read no newspapers at all. But the percentage declines to 1.6 among skilled physical workers. The proportion of workers who read a daily paper rose by over 6.0 per cent since 1965 (75.2 per cent in 1965 and 81.5 per cent in 1970).

Highly-skilled mental workers show a diminishing interest in daily papers over the five years (71.9 per cent in 1965 and 67.7 per cent in 1970), although those reading them irregularly increase by 4.6 per cent. The best newspaper audience among engineering workers in 1970 were supervisors (only 0.4 per cent read no papers at all, and 91.1 per cent read a paper every day). It must be admitted that their intensive reading is probably due as much to the need to keep up with social and political events as part of their social status-maintenance as it is to their general interest in newspapers.

In comparing the changes in reading fiction, it is worth mentioning the drop in readers of one book or more a week over the five years in all groups. Manual workers remain the most avid readers (one book or more a week). Evidently, this may partly be explained by their fixed working day and their correspondingly large amount of free time by comparison with scientific and technical personnel and department heads. All the same, it has to be admitted that 29.2 per cent of workers doing unskilled physical labour read no books at all.

The theatre every year occupies an ever increasing place in the leisure-time of engineering workers. The percentage of people never going to the theatre has diminished in all groups. While nearly 20.0 per cent never visited the theatre in 1965, only 12.2 per cent did not go in 1970. True, we see, too, a slight drop in the number of people visiting the theatre once a month or more, but this is accompanied by a rise in the number of people going to the theatre a few times a year — *i.e.*, approximately once in every six to eight weeks: skilled workers, for example, increased their percentage from 53.8 to 64.8 in 1970.

Information on personal books at home is valuable in forming a picture of the general cultural standards of all grades of worker. It gives us an indication not merely of the cultural level of the worker and his family, but, to a great extent, the whole way of life of Soviet people.

Typically, workers are building up their home libraries. Skilled machine-operators, for example, possessed 60 books on average in 1965, and 73 in 1970; skilled manual physical workers increased their book-stock from 79 to 103. The picture is similar in other groups of engineering workers. We may note that the top department chiefs possess the greatest number of books: over 220 titles on average. Workers employed on jobs requiring a higher education have some 150 books in their home libraries.

Let us turn now to material that shows the number of books among urban families of different nationalities.

These figures, obtained from residents of Kazan, Almetyevsk and Menzelinsk, suggest the following brief conclusions.

(i) The type of town affects the stock of personal books and libraries that people possess. The proportion of families and single people without any books is higher in a small town than in a big city. Thus, 17.3 per cent of Russians and 27.0 per cent of **Tatars*** in Kazan have no books at all, while the figures rise correspondingly to 31.9 and 30.6 per cent in Menzelinsk. The big city also has considerably more families and single persons with small personal libraries. Kazan, for example, has 7.6 per cent of families and single persons among Russians with between 101 and 500 books and 2.4 per cent with over 500 books; the figures for Tatars are 5.5 and 1.6 per cent respectively. In Menzelinsk, however, only 2.6 and 1.9 per cent of Russians and 3.4 and 1.2 per cent of Tatars possess libraries with between 101 and 500 books and over 500 books.

(ii) Social status among both nationalities has a big influence on the number of books a person has: as we move up the occupational scale, so the rise in books and libraries is particularly marked.

---

* Tatars, the fifth largest nationality in the USSR with six million people in 1970, are mainly concentrated in the middle Volga and Urals region where they have their capital at Kazan, once the centre of the Tatar Khanate until it was destroyed by the first Russian tsar Ivan the Terrible. They are descendents of the

(iii) National characteristics are more noticeably in evidence in the big city. Russians in Kazan somewhat surpass Tatars in stock of personal books, while the distribution of books among similar occupational groups of Russians and Tatars is more or less the same in Menzelinsk. The big percentage of both Russians and Tatars with their own books testifies to the high level of culture in these three Tatar towns.

Cultural differences among Russians and Tatars appear to emanate more from social than national factors: education, occupation, residential area.

Let us return to Leningrad engineering workers and examine the role of the cinema and television in their lives.

Clearly, cinema attendance of more than once a week is excessive; it leaves an 'omnivorous' imprint on culture. By comparison with 1965, the proportion of people going to the cinema every week has declined in all groups (from 36.3 to 26.2 per cent among unskilled workers, 56.3 to 52.6 per cent among skilled workers doing mainly physical work handling machines, etc.). At the same time, the percentage of workers visiting cinemas once or twice a month has risen: 50 per cent of highly-skilled workers combining mental and physical jobs went to the cinema once or twice a month in 1970 as against 35.3 per cent in 1965.

The television, which has become an inseparable part of leisure, is an extremely important source of cultural information if only for its extensive range. The largest percentage of undiscriminating viewers of all television programmes are unskilled workers (28.7 per cent). This percentage falls as social status rises, so the specialists with higher education have only 7.5 per cent. The opposite obtains when we look at the figures for viewing interesting programmes only. Some 70.0 per cent of department heads, 64.0 per cent of skilled mental workers, 56.4 per cent of skilled manual physical workers and 39.5 per cent of unskilled workers watch only programmes that interest them.

Besides occupational grade, factors like work record and job-responsibility have considerably influenced cultural and political orientation. The longer the work record, the greater, for example, is the desire to improve political education, to read newspapers regularly and to possess a sizeable home library.

The job-responsibility a person holds also influences cultural and political standards. Movement up the job-responsibility ladder evokes a certain desire to broaden political and cultural erudition. This may be attributable mainly to the increasing feeling of responsibility in performing supervisory functions — *i.e.*, a need to live up to the standard of being a department-head. There is a marked difference in cultural and political standards among the various responsibility-groups. Thus, team-leaders and assistant foremen show considerably lower indices for reading newspapers, political education and home libraries than do foremen and section heads. But the cultural and political level of the latter is slightly lower than that of inspectoral grades in departments, bureaux and laboratories and of administrative personnel in charge of factories, departments and laboratories.

Two exceptions exist — reading books and going to the theatre. Here, individual responsibility at work does not have any noticeable effect; approximately the same figures obtain for all enumerated groups.

The order of influence of the three examined objective factors upon the cultural and political behaviour of engineering workers is as follows: occupation, job-responsibility, work record.

Education also has a considerable bearing on spiritual outlook: rising educational standards clearly affect political and overall cultural standards. On the whole, the cultural indices of all urban groups improve as education increases. This situation is confirmed in regard to reading books, possessing one's own books and going to the theatre.

Having examined cultural values in a big city like Leningrad, let us now look at statistics on use-frequency of certain leisure-forms in Kazan and Menzelinsk (see Table VII).

The information on daily newspapers shows that the majority of residents of Kazan and Menzelinsk, irrespective of nationality, read papers every day or at least acquaint themselves more or less regularly with information from this most mass of all the mass-circulation periodicals. There are no sharp fluctuations in the frequency of newspaper reading according to national differences. The percentage of Russians not reading any papers is 7.8 in Kazan and 10.9 in Menzelinsk; the corresponding figures for Tatars are 10.2 and 6.2 per cent. Russians reading daily papers amount to 57.4 per cent in Kazan and 55.5 per cent in Menzelinsk; the corresponding figures for Tatars are 53.1 and 59.6 per cent respectively.

The figures for book reading, a revealing indicator of cultural values, show that 16.1 per cent of Russians and 24.4 per cent of Tatars in Kazan, 22.7 per cent of Russians and 19.0 per cent of Tatars in Menzelinsk, show absolutely no interest in reading works of fiction. Who actually reads books is of interest, as the following figures reveal. In Kazan, 16.3 per cent of Russians and 11.5 per cent of Tatars read one book or more a week — the figures for Menzelinsk are 20.4 and 14.9 per cent respectively. On the whole, Tatars still lag slightly behind Russians in reading fiction, but the general trend in this very valuable form of leisure is the same. This helps to stimulate an atmosphere of consolidating the interests and friendship of Russians and Tatars.

Going to the cinema is a popular leisure pursuit. Only a tiny section of town-dwellers never go to the cinema: in Kazan, for example, the non-cinema-goers number 7.6 per cent of Russians and 10.8 per cent of Tatars, while in Menzelinsk the corresponding figures are 7.5 and 4.6 per cent. The figures are very high for cinema-goers who make no fewer than one or two outings a month. As many as 72.2 per cent of Russians and 66.4 per cent of Tatars in Kazan, 69.4 per cent of Russians and 79.9 per cent of Tatars in Menzelinsk, go no less than once or twice a month, or once a week or more. As we see, frequency of cinema-going is higher among Tatars in the smaller town than in the Republican capital. Intensive cinema-going, whereby the different nationalities see one and the same film programme, undoubtedly forges a cultural contact and helps to bring the socialist nationalities together culturally.

Table VII

Use-Frequency of Leisure-Forms in Kazan and Menzelinsk 1967
(people questioned according to each factor)

Leisure-form	Use-frequency of given form of leisure	Russians Kazan	Russians Menzelinsk	Tatars Kazan	Tatars Menzelinsk
Reading newspapers	Not at all	7.8	10.9	10.2	6.2
	Not every day	34.4	33.6	36.5	33.7
	Every day	57.4	55.5	53.1	59.6
	No reply	0.4	-	0.2	0.5
Reading books (fiction)	Not at all	16.1	22.7	24.4	19.0
	No fewer than 1 a month	29.2	23.6	35.0	31.8
	1-2 books a month	37.5	32.7	28.5	33.7
	1 or more books a week	16.3	20.4	11.5	14.9
	No reply	0.9	0.6	0.6	0.6
Cinema-going	Do not normally go	7.6	7.5	10.8	4.6
	A few times a year	19.6	23.1	22.3	14.9
	1-2 a month	33.7	30.4	30.5	36.8
	Once a week or more	38.5	39.0	35.9	43.1
	No reply	0.6	-	0.5	0.6
Going to the theatre and concert hall	Not at all	21.8	26.8	21.0	16.8
	A few times a year	66.4	60.7	62.9	63.7
	No less than once a month	11.8	11.4	15.1	18.7
	No reply	-	1.1	1.0	0.8

The picture is somewhat different in regard to theatre-going. Both national groups have a sizeable proportion of persons who never go to see a theatrical or concert performance. As many as 21.8 per cent of Russians and 21.0 per cent of Tatars never go to the theatre in Kazan, and 26.8 and 16.8 per cent respectively never go in Menzelinsk. Figures showing regular theatre-goers are less impressive. Thus, 11.8 per cent of Russians and 15.1 per cent of Tatars go to the theatre no less than once a month in Kazan — the corresponding figures for Menzelinsk being 11.4 and 18.7 per cent. Interestingly enough, Tatars are ahead of Russians in theatre-attendance. The overwhelming majority of people in the two towns visit the theatre a few times a year, and this does not appear to be sharply influenced by nationality or residential district.

In establishing a dependence between different cultural forms, it is natural that the force of influence of the factors determining consumption should vary. To analyse the most meaningful factors determining cultural interests, we thought it expedient to construct matrices. We explain this on the example of Table VIII.[44] It is clear that education is the main factor affecting cultural values.

Certain specific characteristics are naturally highlighted in interpreting these questions. Thus, interest in the theatre in all our surveys was found to be greatest among people with complete secondary and higher education. How do we explain this? Does it establish a pattern? In our view, the research undertaken does not allow us to answer these questions with any authority. We can only put forward the hypothesis that aesthetic appreciation is not the same for all educational groups. The desire for aesthetic knowledge may, on the one hand, be due to lack of erudition and an urge to broaden one's cultural outlook. On the other, it may be due to the enhanced selective ability of people with a high level of aesthetic appreciation. The former will show a desire to enjoy all means of aesthetic appreciation to the maximum, while the latter will only use those channels which enable them to deepen existing knowledge.

We have established that urban culture depends to a considerable extent on the occupation group to which one belongs; the higher up the ladder one goes, the higher the cultural standards. We ought to emphasise, however, that this is not a simple process or one of a single order. One and the same person, for example, is influenced by not one but several channels of the mass media and there is no uniformity in their use. A cultural form may give satisfaction to one person and be boring to someone else. Obviously, the choice of a particular cultural channel very much depends, too, on an individual's specific social role, his occupational group. This circumstance stimulates, in turn, a need to differentiate among the mass media, which vary both in content and in the nature of the information being transmitted. This ought to be taken into account in any practical work that aspires to improve the mass media. And this, in turn, requires a specific historical approach, a genuinely scientific account of economic, social and cultural conditions, all the intricacies and contradictions that arise.

Our material testifies to the equal opportunities for different urban occupational groups to improve their general cultural standards. The ways and means of

Table VIII

Dependence of Cultural Consumption on Social and Demographic Factors, 1967 (in Chuprov coefficients)

Socio demographic factors	Town	Possess books	Go to the theatre	Read (fiction) books	Read news-papers	Listen to music	Go to the cinema	Attend clubs, houses of culture	Watch TV
Education	Kazan	0.235	0.159	0.197	0.198	0.134	0.179	0.108	0.115
	Almetyevsk	0.199	0.159	0.186	0.206	0.139	0.171	0.124	0.089
	Menzelinsk	0.261	0.130	0.217	0.244	0.137	0.160	0.127	0.127
Occupational structure	Kazan	0.188	0.127	0.125	0.166	0.144	0.130	0.084	0.109
	Almetyevsk	0.181	0.117	0.142	0.170	0.153	0.118	0.101	0.091
	Menzelinsk	0.190	0.140	0.158	0.172	0.135	0.127	0.151	0.125
Age	Kazan	0.084	0.099	0.146	0.092	0.101	0.205	0.149	0.089
	Almetyevsk	.....	.....	0.124	0.106	0.134	0.188	0.130	0.091
	Menzelinsk	0.107	0.090	0.159	0.125	0.131	0.149	0.078	0.078
Nationality	Almetyevsk	0.085	0.032	0.074	0.060	.....	0.019	0.031	0.045

satisfying the cultural demands of the working class and other strata of the urban population are, on the whole, of a rational order; by this we understand the broad and all-round satisfaction by people of their cultural requirements. There are, of course, several deviations. Shortcomings in this field may come from objective and subjective factors which are inextricably bound up with one another.

The steady rise in the consumption of various types of cultural values by different social strata and urban groups undoubtedly helps to stimulate the production and socio-political affairs of the country; that is an important condition for the further successful construction of communism in the USSR.

3. Family life

The family — the primary cell of everyday life — occupies a prominent place in the complex process of building the foundation of the new way of life.

The modern urban family conventionally consists of two generations — *i.e.*, spouses and children. Families of more than three generations are extremely rare in cities. Big changes are taking place in worker-families, since many now include both physical labourers and intellectuals, thereby making it hard to define their social membership. According to the survey of Leningrad engineering workers, carried out in 1970, between 14.1 and 17.7 per cent of adult children in all groups of manual workers became employees with a complete specialised secondary education, and between 5.8 and 10.4 per cent gained a higher education. A large number of workers' children were at college or university. The families of skilled workers engaged mainly on handling machinery and of skilled workers doing mainly manual physical labour had 23.7 and 24.0 per cent of their children studying, respectively. At the same time, families of unskilled and low-grade physical and mental workers without specialist training had only 5.2 per cent of their children in higher education.

It would therefore seem a fundamentally new phenomenon for today's workers to have their own intellectuals in their midst; what is less common is for a stratum of manual workers to exist in an intellectual milieu. This development helps further to promote and consolidate social and cultural unity within society. In such mixed families, members of the older generation come under the influence of young people, read a great deal and often go to the cinema or theatre. Young people, in turn, take over the class-political experience of their parents. All this encourages a mutual cultural enrichment of all family members and supplements their knowledge. In this connection, it is apposite to point out that under socialism there can be no conflict between the older and younger generations, such as occurs, according to some bourgeois writers, in capitalist countries.[45] The existence of an intellectual stratum within worker-families helps greatly to overcome any deleterious vestiges of the past (particularly religious) that some members may still cling to; they can best be combatted within the family itself.

From none of this may we infer that a 'levelling out' is taking place in everyday life and familial relations. It cannot do so because of the unimaginable complexity of socialist transformation in the economy, in the minds and spiritual

Table IX

Size of Family, Average Size of Family, Average Number of
Family-Members with an Independent Source of Income, and
Average Age of Leningrad Engineering Workers, Related to
Occupational Group, 1965

Group by nature of work	Of which possess a family (%) consisting of (no.)						Average size of family	Average number of family-members with an independent source of income	Average age of persons questioned (years)
	1	2	3	4	5 and more	Total			
1. Unskilled physical workers..........	15.9	19.3	35.4	21.8	7.6	100	2.89	2.21	39.2
2. Low-grade mental workers..........	9.7	25.2	32.5	22.0	10.6	100	3.04	2.32	32.2
3. Skilled workers doing mainly physical labour handling machinery.	15.6	22.5	35.9	17.1	10.9	100	2.93	2.15	35.7
4. Skilled workers doing mainly manual physical work......	7.4	18.5	34.9	28.2	11.0	100	3.23	2.28	39.1
5. Highly-skilled workers combining physical and mental jobs.............	6.1	16.9	35.6	21.6	19.8	100	3.42	2.54	35.3
6. Skilled mental workers...........	10.7	20.4	38.9	21.0	10.0	100	3.03	2.34	36.8
7. Highly-skilled scientific and technical personnel.........	6.2	22.5	33.6	21.6	14.1	100	3.18	2.43	35.7
8. Supervisors........	9.5	15.9	39.6	22.7	12.3	100	3.18	2.25	41.8
Total	10.1	20.0	35.8	21.9	12.2	100	3.12	2.32	36.9

life of millions of people; the complexity is also part of our attempt to resolve completely new tasks that have no historical prototype. In so far as socialism does not suddenly appear ready-made, but emerges from the womb of capitalism, a certain inequality will long remain under socialism in the distribution of the social product and in personal consumption. This inequality therefore has an objective basis.

Material illustrating the size of families in different occupational groups is of considerable interest in our study of the many facets of family life. We reproduce data on size of family, number of members with independent earnings and the average age of the persons questioned (in 1965) in Table IX.[46]

The figures show that family composition varies although families of three-four members predominate in all groups. Families of two members are least likely in the supervisory groups (15.9 per cent) and among highly-skilled workers combining mental and physical work (16.9 per cent). The greatest number of two-person families is among low-grade mental workers (25.2 per cent) and highly-skilled scientific and technical personnel (22.5 per cent).

Families with more than five members appear most often in the highly-skilled groups that combine mental and physical jobs (some 20 per cent). It is noteworthy that the lowest percentage of such families (7.6) occurs among unskilled workers. Meanwhile, highly-skilled mental workers and supervisory groups have a higher percentage of families with five or more members than all other groups, save the above-mentioned highly-skilled workers.

Occupational grades ranged according to family size, members with independent earnings and age give us an idea of the number of dependents. Groups at opposite ends of the scale (unskilled and supervisors) take first place in age. They differ in average family composition: 2.89 (unskilled) and 3.18 (supervisors), but are more or less identical in number of family-members with their own independent earnings (2.12 and 2,25); this, of course, affects the number of dependents. If we compare supervisory grades with skilled workers doing mainly manual work – *i.e.*, groups whose average age is very similar (41.8 and 39.1), we see that there is actually no difference in number of dependents; that is due to the near identical average family size and number of persons with an independent source of income. The average age of skilled workers doing mainly physical labour handling machinery and of highly-skilled scientific and technical personnel coincides; they, too, show insignificant differences in number of dependents despite the different family make-up and number of members with independent earnings. Although the average age of unskilled workers is virtually the highest, they have the lowest number of dependents. That would indicate not only the large number of people with independent earnings, but also the smallest number of children in their families. It is difficult to see any increase in size of family coming from this group in the future. So we have a situation in which the lowest occupational group evidently has the lowest number of children at whose expense the basic contingent of dependents is actually formed.

Further, we must dwell on family-members with independent earnings by way of permanent wages, pensions, student grants, etc. Elucidation of this question is crucial to an understanding of family structure — *i.e.*, the character of family relations, role-distribution between spouses, and 'democratisation' of the family structure. To tackle this problem properly, we should, besides political and legal aspects, seriously take account of economic relations in the urban family.

The process of democratising the family, above all the urban family, is regretfully not reflected accurately in the budget surveys of the USSR Central Statistical Board, in which social membership is defined by the social group to which a family member within the sample belongs. This approach is incorrect from the methodological standpoint, inasmuch as we are witnessing today, as seen above, a differing social affiliation among members of the same families. The error in such methods of analysis may be traced to the fact that they have been mechanically adopted from pre-revolutionary practice.

The issue of the democratising process underway within a Soviet worker-family has not yet received proper treatment in learned publications; account has to be taken of the entire complex system of inner-family relations. We mention below just a few basic factors that shape the structure of the family.

The first meaningful index is the number of persons within a family who are working. Leningrad engineering workers had a very high percentage of family-members with independent earnings (74 on average) in 1965 and 1970. It is noteworthy that in all families the share of people with a permanent source of income is no less than 70 per cent. The highest number of those with independent earnings belongs to unskilled workers, who make up 79 per cent of the total number of families on this count. The figures for 1965 are also of interest in that they show the number of members of families with independent earnings by all categories of Leningrad engineering workers related to size of family (see Table X).

The greatest number of people with independent earnings is recorded in families of two or three persons. But even in larger families, the number of independent earners does not fall below 65-66 per cent.

The figures in tables IX and X are of prime importance from the standpoint of social integration; families differing in size and in social affiliation have several members who go out to work. Our calculations show that the proportion of people working fluctuates between 70 and 79 per cent of the total number of

Table X
Number of Family-Members with Independent Earnings Related to Size of Family (persons), 1965

Size of family	With independent earnings
one	1.0
two	1.9
three	2.2

four	2.6
five	3.3
six and over	4.0

families in the survey within different occupational groups. These fluctuations indicate the great burden that falls upon working family-members both of manual worker-families and of other families that we have examined. Vital processes are evidently at work among Leningrad families leading to the convergence of intra-class groups through the family cell.

The fairly high number of urban family-members with their own independent earnings is not encouraging the establishment of a hierarchical family structure. Of course, the figures cannot provide a complete picture of the urban family structure. We must trace the life-journey of children, related to their parents' profession, which interests us here not in general terms but more from the standpoint of classifying industrial workers into social groups — from auxiliary labourers to highly-skilled personnel. Additionally, we should use material illustrating the interrelationship between the job-responsibility of the parent and the social status of his or her grown-up children.

Some information on this question is cited above. The results of the 1965 and 1970 Leningrad surveys also confirm that no occupational uniformity is observable within manual-worker families. In all groups of manual workers, especially the skilled, about half their children had become engineering and technical personnel, employees and students. This is clear evidence that in socialist conditions, when antagonistic classes no longer exist, occupational differences shed their former contradictions. True, we cannot ignore the fact that only 15.1 and 13.2 per cent of the children of designers in 1965 and 1970 respectively were doing physical labour. In addition, a considerable number of children within that group were doing physical work merely as a temporary measure — because, for example, they had failed to get into higher education that year. Over 80 per cent of children of that category acquired a mental skill in 1965, of whom 48.7 per cent became engineering and technical personnel and 18.1 per cent were studying in higher or secondary educational institutions. Interestingly enough, only 9.1 per cent of the children of designers were students of the humanities. The picture had hardly changed in 1970.

Vocational inclinations may be perceived as social inclinations — *i.e.*, a desire to remain within the same social group or to move to another. The children of designers would seem to be acquiring a trade that enables them to stay in the same social group of their parents; on the other hand, children of manual workers show a tendency to move to a different social group, one associated with the performance of social functions of mental workers.

There is an essential distinction between trades acquired by the children of manual workers and those obtained by the children of intellectuals. At the same time, opportunities do exist for a really free choice of trade (that is confirmed by the above-quoted figures), for moving from one occupational group to

Table XI

Job-Responsibility of Wife (Husband) in Relation to that of Husband (Wife) among Leningrad Engineering Workers, 1965

Trade of those questioned	What the wife (husband) does (%)								Total
	Manual Worker	Technician	Other Workers with Secondary Education	Engineer	Other Workers with Higher Education	Employee of other Categories	Student	Housewife	
Auxiliary worker	62.3	15.5	4.2	1.3	2.8	5.6	1.3	7.0	100
Machine-operatore	57.9	7.0	8.2	3.5	2.9	15.9	1.1	3.5	100
Machine-mechanic	57.2	8.4	9.1	3.0	2.4	14.5	1.8	3.6	100
Fitter	50.3	9.5	8.5	3.5	2.1	18.3	2.1	5.7	100
Flow-line operator	53.6	6.9	16.3	2.3	4.6	16.3	0.0	0.0	100
Designer	13.2	14.6	13.3	37.7	8.1	8.1	2.0	3.0	100

another. Social mobility in socialist conditions obviously is fundamentally different from 'mobility' in capitalist states where opportunities to move up the social ladder are extremely limited. Mobility in socialist society is related to scientific and technical progress, the continual erosion of the boundaries between mental and physical work, increasing material welfare for all people and certain other factors.

To appreciate the causes of wider democracy within the worker-family, we must consult data (for 1965) that tell us what work husbands and wives actually do (see Table XI).

The first item of note is that just over 59 per cent of the spouses of manual workers are themselves employed in manual work. But the overall trend is for the number of spouses doing manual work to decline as we move up the occupational scale. Thus, 62.3 per cent of auxiliary workers have both spouses engaged in manual labour, while the proportion falls to 53.6 and 50.3 per cent respectively for flow-line operators and fitters. It is noteworthy, too, that only 13.2 per cent of the spouses of designers are engaged on manual work, while the rest, save a small percentage of housewives, are engineering and technical personnel, employees or students in colleges and tekhnikums. Their percentage of engineers and other professions with higher education is particularly high (45.8). Meanwhile, skilled manual workers (machine-operators and metal-cutting machine-mechanics,flow-line operators, etc.) record a more or less equal number of spouses belonging to engineering and technical personnel and to other trades demanding a full secondary or higher education.

We have relied here on data indicating only the most representative groups of manual workers and employees in relation to the nature of their work. A deeper analysis would seem to require am examination of material revealing what job the husband or wife does in relation to the job-responsibility of the person questioned. On the basis of our survey of Leningrad engineering workers in 1965 we established that the husband or wife of 59.2 per cent of all manual workers is also a manual worker. If we exclude the 4.8 per cent of housewives we are left with 36 per cent who are engineering or technical personnel, employees, students and other people with a full secondary or higher education; most are, in fact, employees or technical workers, with engineers and other non-manual workers with higher education comprising 3.6 and 2.3 per cent respectively. The situation is different among brigade-leaders and assistant foremen: they have only 42.9 per cent of spouses belonging to manual groups, while the remainder, excluding 6.7 per cent who are housewives, are employed on mental work. It is interesting that among brigade-leaders and manual workers, there are large groups of husbands or wives working as technicians and employees; brigade-leaders, however, show far more spouses who are engineers than do ordinary manual workers.

Highly-skilled scientific and technical personnel and supervisory grades show a relatively small percentage of husbands or wives doing mainly physical labour; most spouses are engineering and technical personnel or employees. True, managerial groups have a relatively large group of housewives – 11 per cent against 3.9 per cent for supervisors of departments, bureaux or laboratories. The number of spouses working as employees in these groups is virtually the same — 13.0 and 13.3 per cent.

Table XI allows us to assert the following; first, the choice of a wife or husband still evidently very much depends on occupational group; secondly, in many manual worker-families, the husband or wife is engaged in mental work; thirdly, skilled manual workers and employees with a complete secondary specialised education have the greatest number of mixed families.

The above-mentioned propositions bring us to yet another problem that merits the most careful consideration. Inasmuch as relations between husband and wife are crucial to family relations, no less important is the question of who is head of the family; this question affects in essence the whole intricate set of relations between spouses. The modern urban family does not have a head of the family in the true meaning of the term, because the status of spouses is equal both in a socio-economic and in a moral sense. As we know, before the revolution the man was invariably head of the family and his domination was never disputed. The loss of male supremacy in the family in Soviet times is attributable, among other things, to the equal rights of husband and wife in regard to property and to the existing wide opportunities for free choice of occupation based on the personal aspirations of both partners.

From his sociological research among Leningrad workers in the early 1960's, A.G. Kharchev concluded that no less than 60 per cent of families had firmly established *de facto* equality of partners, and approximately 36 per cent of families had retained the man as head of the family, although, in four out of five cases, it was a purely nominal post.[47] From the Kharchev data, therefore, we may assume that personal power within the family is actually retained in a few worker-families (no more than 8 per cent). Apparently, families still exist among manual workers where the family is headed by the man and, not infrequently, by the woman. Despite the fact that this question is still to some extent debatable, it would seem that under socialism the nature of family headship has altered even in families which retain a head. The overall trend in family relations is for the husband completely to forfeit his absolute role as head of the family; the end to male domination in the family is having a favourable effect on the overall character of family relations.

Any serious attempt to study the structure of a worker-family must, of course, include a look at the position of women. On the basis of existing material and our personal observations of domestic life of workers at the Leningrad S.M. Kirov *Elektrosila* plant, we may emphasise the fact of equality of men and women. At the same time, it must be said that male supremacy had not been rampant even in the pre-revolutionary worker-family. The proletarian family even before 1917 had differed from the bourgeois family, based as it was on economic interest. Workers had tended to conclude their marriages on the basis of mutual affection and love. The woman in a worker-family had been more equal and had enjoyed greater respect from her husband and other members of the family than had the woman in a bourgeois or peasant family.

Women in worker-families under capitalism, however, do not obtain full equality even when they become more independent — because of the social system. As Lenin put it: "In no capitalist state, even the freest republic, is there complete equality of women."[48] Economic and legal conditions in addition to the whole tenor of life force women ultimately into a subordinate status, dependent upon their husbands.

The status of women altered drastically in Russia after the Great October Socialist Revolution. One of the prime tasks of Soviet government had been "as first priority to abolish all restrictions on women's rights."[49] It is true that in the immediate post-revolutionary years, women could not obtain *de facto* equality with men because, until the late 1920's, they were little involved in production and lagged a long way behind men in vocational training. That made women economically dependent on men. Other deleterious factors were their low level of literacy and the overwhelming burden of domestic work. Old vestiges and traditions that survived among workers also had militated against genuine equal rights between men and women. Today, women in our society enjoy equal economic, legal and political rights with men. Such a situation affects not only the equality, but the prestige of women within the family, and encourages women to appreciate their own personal worth.

By equality we understand the provision of equal opportunities with men for women to improve their qualifications, obtain an education, take on job-responsibility and, primarily, to receive equal payment for equal work.

Every opportunity exists in the USSR, as a matter of principle, for everyone to obtain and improve qualifications. On the whole, qualification standards of working men are still higher than those of women.[50] At the same time, the Leningrad example clearly shows a trend towards equality among the sexes in vicational training. We agree with Leningrad researchers into manpower mobility at industrial enterprises when they say: "When a young girl finds herself in the same conditions as men she masters a trade no less rapidly than men do. Once she reaches the 21-25 age range, however, she does not improve her qualifications as rapidly because she has the burden of family responsibility on her shoulders. This has nothing to do with any specific characteristics of her sex; it is because of the inadequate development of consumer services, insufficient assistance within the family, and so on." [51]

Soviet women have a reasonably high level of education for which they enjoy equal opportunities with men. Moreover, in certain respects women come even higher than men in extent of education.

The high level of female education naturally leads to a situation where they occupy responsible positions, from ordinary manual workers to managerial responsibility for factories, workshops, departments, bureaux and laboratories. It is true that, for the time being, men still show a higher percentage in all these positions. A large number of women today possess a skilled trade and are performing jobs that require a high degree of knowledge. Women are now doing work that used to employ very limited female labour. Today we are attracting women into production considerably faster than in capitalist states where women's access to skilled jobs is very restricted.[52] Of course, we do not mean in any way to belittle the importance of the mother-role, bringing up and tutoring the younger generation. Here, incidentally, we find a certain contradiction between women's functions in social production and their functions as mothers and housewives.

We have now arrived at the problem of the status of working women in everyday life. A study of the vast material that lies behind this work convinces us that we in this country still tend to overburden the working mother with housework. That is particularly apparent when we examine time budget studies, as we do in the next chapter.

Women bear the main burden also in bringing up children. In many cases, they receive no adequate assistance from other members of the family. Some manual workers frequently say categorically that their wives are mainly responsible for the children.

Data on Leningrad engineering workers give some idea of the obstacles in the way of women who wish to study. The main obstacles to women continuing studies, besides age and ill health, are care of children and housework. In 1965, 16.4 and 10.8 per cent of women gave these reasons for not studying, against 8.2 and 3 per cent of men.

The problem of the domestic status of women is exceedingly complex and merits special examination.[53] We shall therefore only note in passing that many men would seem to need enlightening so that they share the child-rearing work with their wives. If men were to take an active part in looking after children and doing housework, this could help to make women's status equal with men in everyday life. When young workers marry they are usually ill-informed about family life and Soviet family legislation because they receive practically no information about it in school or any other educational establishment. Not enough popular literature on these problems is published. In our view, young people should be better informed at school or college about marriage and the family. That would undoubtedly help to create a genuinely equal basis for relations between spouses in bringing up children and doing housework. It would also have a beneficial effect on improving polite and considerate behaviour, etc. This is all the more important, since, according to A.G. Zdravomyslov and V.Y. Yadov, the family occupies an extremely important place in the value-orientations of young workers.[54]

Let us make a few comments on bringing up the younger generation. This aspect of everyday life gives us an idea of how social and family elements of everyday life are combined. Children of pre-school age particularly interest us. We can look at this on the example of Menzelinsk, which is a fairly small town. We should note at once that type of town does not significantly affect child upbringing. Only 10.7 per cent of pre-school children in Menzelinsk remain at home, the rest going to creches and kindergartens (including 24-hour nurseries). This shows once again that no other country in the world manifests such care for the all-round physical and spiritual development of children as the USSR. Specially-trained teachers provide children with all their meals, rest, play and care in the pre-school institutions.*

The data on pre-school education show that the proportion of home-based children declines as we mount the occupational scale. Thus, 21.0 per cent of the children of skilled manual workers handling machinery are brought up at home, against 7.4 per cent of the children of skilled mental workers. Highly-skilled workers have fewer children in nurseries than do manual labourers. The large percentage of nursery-based children in all occupational groups in Menzelinsk has a not inconsiderable effect on the communist upbringing of the younger generation. Several years ago, N.K. Krupskaya* emphasised that "a wonderful generation of people is growing up by combining family upbringing with the public education we give in our pre-school institutions and schools." [55]

Much has been done in recent years to improve housing construction and communal services. [56] Nonetheless, it is clear that the time being spent by women on housework is still great, despite the widespread building of new flats with all modern conveniences, the availability of many labour-saving domestic appliances, extensive communal services and, finally, the limited help that women receive from other members of the family. The 24th Party Congress Ninth Five-Year Plan Directives provide for substantial improvement in communal services by extending and mechanising all such services: the total volume of consumer services throughout the USSR is to more than double in the space of five years, 1971-75.[57]

Under socialism, a family-type considerably depends on housing conditions which, in turn, affect social relations in everyday life. So it is valuable to examine information that tells us where people meet their friends. The home would appear to be about equal with the workplace in meeting friends. Most friendship ties (over 60.0 per cent) were established either at work or at home, as surveys in Kazan, Almetyevsk and Menzelinsk show.

A clear pattern does seem to emerge: the proportion of Russians and Tatars who began friendships at place of residence significantly diminishes as we go up the occupational scale, especially in the big city. For example, 33.4 per cent of Russians, and 33.4 per cent of Tatars in Kazan who had struck up a friendship at their place of residence were skilled manual workers handling machinery; corres-

---

* Creches (*yasli*) were for children aged one to three, kindergartens (*detskiy sad*) for the four-, five, and six-year olds, compulsory schooling starting at age seven. After 1971, these two pre-school institutions were combined into *yasli-sady*. They are neither free (though the charge is minimal) nor compulsory, but with most mothers working they accommodate the majority of eligible children in most areas.

* Nadezhda Krupskaya (1869-1939), wife of Lenin and eminent educationalist in her own right.

ponding figures for mental workers of both nationalities are 17.2 and 13.0 per cent respectively. Additionally, many mental workers make friends while studying: 23.8 per cent of Russians and 24.7 per cent of Tatars doing skilled mental work got to know their friends while students. These figures rise by an average of 7.0 per cent for Russians and Tatars alike in supervisory grades in industrial, public and state organisations.

Evidently, place of residence has considerable importance for starting friendship ties, which provides an objective social basis for bringing together town-dwellers of similar and dissimilar social and national groups. Friendship-formation at place of residence is a form of social contact within the town unconnected with work and affecting the formation of a uniform structure of everyday life. Social groups are interacting with others and intermixing different cultural attitudes.

The socialist system has had a decisive impact on the old form of everyday life, has given it a new socialist form and has stimulated changes in urban family life, above all in that of the manual worker-family. Today the moral aspect plays a dominant part in family relations among the various strata and groups of the urban population. The socialist system has brought the complete disappearance of many old mores and traditions based on religious canons and the economic oppression of women. Communist morality is now the moral foundation of the Soviet family; it combines personal and public life into a single whole and helps to shape the basis both of everyday life and of the entire Soviet way of life.

Chapter 4

Cumulative Methods of Investigating Everyday Life

1. Time-budgets as a concentrated expression of everyday life

Given the present duration of the working day, working time comprises no more than 33.3 per cent of the aggregate 24-hour time-fund for most Soviet people. The remaining time is non-working time. It is used for satisfying physiological requirements — *i.e.*, on restoring expended physical and mental effort, studying, improving qualifications, self-education, rest, entertainment, etc. Since it takes up as much as 70 per cent of a person's life and expresses the basic features of everyday life, non-working time has immense social significance.

Before looking at certain aspects of everyday life according to time-structure, we shall first make a few comments on the methodology of our present investigation. We made our first time-budget use survey in the summer of 1966 on the recommendation of the Leningrad City Party Committee. The survey encompassed eight large enterprises (including the Kirov) and three research institutes. The data collected by self-registration were put on time-expenditure calculation cards and then processed at the Leningrad Mechanised Calculation Institute of the RSFSR Central Statistical Board.[1] Registration of time-expenditure over a week of observation was confined to two week days — immediately before the day off and the day off itself. We selected persons at the factories and institutes by random cluster sampling according to the nature of their work; we obtained 2,564 24-hour time-budgets in all.[2]

We also had at our disposal time-budgets obtained in the summer of 1968 at the Leningrad Kalinin *Skorokhod* factory. As with the previous survey, time-fund material was collected by self-registration — *i.e.*, a detailed (with an exactitude of up to 3-5 minutes) record of all actual time-expenditure — filled in during a week in July 1968 by the person questioned, supervised by a public instructor. The selection of persons in workshops and other factory departments was made by random cluster sampling according to nature of work. Altogether, 2,389 24-hour time-budgets were available. Selection of units of observation in each workshop or department within the sample was random but not unsystematic. The public instructor gave all participants instructions, carried out a daily check on the record and transmitted the information to time-expenditure calculation cards which, as in 1966, were processed at the Leningrad Mechanised Calculation Institute of the RSFSR Central Statistical Board.

As the basis of investigation the researchers took a select group of industrial workers classified by the nature and content of their work.

In drawing the public into compiling time-budgets, the *Skorokhod* Scientific Labour Organisation office, which carried out the survey, proceeded from Lenin's dictum that "statistics in capitalist society have been a subject dealt with exclusively by bureaucrats or narrow specialists; we must bring them to the common people, popularise them so that the working people gradually realise and see how to work, how much work to do, how to rest and how much rest to have." [3]

Information obtained from the *Skorokhod* survey enables us, among other things, to trace changes in time-allocation after the change-over to the five-day week.

We do not have space to reproduce data characterising all our research, so we shall confine ourselves to overall time-fund structure and free-time budgets, using only the variable magnitudes most relevant for the purposes of our study. These comprise nature of work, sex and family situation. Since, in characterising all non-working time, we cannot rely solely on general and average figures that are typical, say, of a weekly time-budget, we produce here budgets showing the allocation of time during a working day and a day off.

Let us look now at the figures showing total time-fund use related to nature of work and sex during a working-day (see Table XII).

The table reveals that duration of the working day is not the same for all workers. Some categories of worker have slightly more actual working time than that officially prescribed. Thus, highly-skilled working men combining mental and physical jobs work nearly eight out of every 24 hours, while skilled men and women doing mainly manual physical work do just over seven hours work a day. Of course, if we were to compare the 24-hour time-budget (shown in Table XII) with a weekly time-budget, we should see that highly-skilled men work between two and four-and-a-half hours more than the set weekly norm.

In regard to mental and non-physical workers, all categories, with the exception of women doing skilled mental work, actually work more than the norm; this is patently apparent with supervisors of both sexes and men employed on highly-skilled scientific and technical work.

No more than 36 per cent of total budget-time is spent on satisfying natural physiological needs. This is a constant magnitude that is unlikely to alter in the future. In certain cases, however, women spend rather more time than men on satisfying their natural physiological needs. This may well be due to the fact that the study was conducted in summer when many married women had sent their children out of town for the summer holidays, so granting the working mothers a considerable reserve of additional time. If we compare our data (24-hour and weekly surveys) with the time-budgets of men and women surveyed in Leningrad in 1961, there are no noticeable deviations in time spent on satisfying natural physiological needs.[4]

Expenditure related to work but not having a direct bearing on working time comprises between 5.4 and 8.8 per cent of the total time-fund. These figures testify to differential time expenditure under this item among different occupational grades. No distinct pattern of use of work-related non-working time is discernible by sex, but it is apparent that highly-skilled scientific and technical personnel, particularly men, spend more time than other groups on travelling to

Table XII

Utilisation of Total Time-Fund on a Working Day, Related to Nature of Work and Sex, 1966
(in minutes and as a percentage of the total time fund*)

Groups by nature of work	Sex	Working time		Non-working time connected with work		Type of time-expenditure Housework		Satisfaction of natural physiological needs		Free time	
		min.	%	min.	%	min.	%	min.	%	min.	%
1. Unskilled physical workers	men	433.7	30.1	82.6	5.7	147.9	10.3	516.6	35.9	259.2	18.0
	women	424.7	29.5	88.9	6.2	291.0	20.2	490.5	34.0	144.9	10.1
2. Low-grade mental workers	men	435.0	30.2	103.0	7.1	130.3	9.1	488.5	33.9	283.2	19.7
	women	439.4	30.5	87.5	6.1	252.3	17.5	497.7	34.6	163.1	11.3
3. Skilled workers (mainly physical) handling machinery	men	429.6	29.8	109.1	7.6	112.8	7.8	506.2	35.2	282.3	19.6
	women	428.3	29.7	85.9	6.0	218.5	15.2	502.0	34.9	205.3	14.2
4. Skilled workers doing mainly manual work	men	438.4	30.4	88.5	6.1	141.9	9.9	484.6	33.6	286.6	20.0
	women	453.5	31.5	78.8	5.5	218.4	15.2	489.1	33.9	200.2	13.9
5. Highly-skilled workers combining physical and mental work	men	475.2	33.0	101.6	7.1	114.1	7.9	503.5	34.9	245.6	17.1
	women	424.4	29.5	108.5	7.5	234.9	16.3	505.7	35.1	166.5	11.6
6. Skilled mental workers	men	445.6	30.9	92.3	6.4	110.6	7.7	495.0	34.4	296.5	20.6
	women	426.1	29.6	97.3	6.8	236.7	16.4	510.3	35.4	169.6	11.8
7. Highly-skilled mental workers	men	454.6	31.5	126.2	8.8	122.1	8.6	503.6	34.9	233.6	16.2
	women	430.9	29.9	109.9	7.6	233.3	15.2	485.6	33.8	180.3	12.5
8. Supervisors	men	509.0	35.3	103.8	7.2	102.5	7.1	494.1	34.4	230.6	16.0
	women	487.4	33.8	77.8	5.4	212.3	14.7	476.7	33.2	185.8	12.9

* The total time-fund was 1440 mins.

work and back. By virtue of the nature of their work, this category would seem to enjoy a comparatively limited opportunity to choose a workplace in the vicinity of their place of residence. They therefore show a relatively high time-expenditure on work-related functions. The greatest travel-time is spent by workers living on new estates which are normally remote from many industrial undertakings and offices located inside the old metropolitan area.

Working women in all categories have to bear an especially heavy burden in regard to housework. Working men spend almost half as much time as women on housework, the only exception being skilled workers doing mainly physical work where the gap is reduced to 65 per cent. The principle burden of caring for children, cleaning, laundry, etc., is also borne by women. But not all men react uniformly to housework: those who devote least time to housework are supervisors — 7.1 per cent of the total time-budget. Among manual workers, the participation of men in housework vacillates from 7.8 per cent among skilled workers handling machinery to 10.3 per cent among unskilled workers. Among working women, time spent on housework ranges from 14.7 to 20.2 per cent of their time-budget. Women on average spend about four hours each day on housework. Unskilled manual working women spend most time on housework (4.8 hours a day).

Every worker in socialist society has the right to free time, granted to him by the USSR Constitution. This is a feature of the nature of the socialist system in which all working people enjoy equal status in regard to the means of production, enjoy equality in work and equal pay for equal work. Yet this cannot preclude disparities of free-time use among categories of workers.

Free time constitutes from 10.1 to 20.0 per cent of the time budget of all workers. Just a glance at the figures, however, is sufficient to show that men enjoy considerably more free time than women. While unskilled men have as much as 18 per cent of their time free, women of the same category have only 10.1 per cent.. The situation is virtually the same with highly-skilled and skilled manual workers. The smallest gulf between men and women in access to free time is among skilled manual workers handling machinery: here free time amounts to 19.6 and 14.2 per cent respectively of the total time-fund.

A marked trend is evident in reduction of the free-time gulf between men and women among highly-skilled scientific and technical personnel and supervisors. True, this is partly because men are helping more with housework and partly because of less actual working time and non-working time related to work.

Time spent on the day off has its own specific characteristics (see Table XIII). Here we are dealing with three groups of time expenditure only: housework, satisfaction of natural physiological needs and free time. We should note first of all that the share of time spent by men on housework increases in all occupational groups on the day off. On the other hand, the women's housework time-expenditure remains the same or even diminishes slightly by comparison with the working day. The only exceptions are women working on highly-skilled scientific

Table XIII
Utilisation of Non-Working Time on Day Off, Related to Nature of Work and Sex, 1966
(in minutes and as a percentage of the total time fund)

	Groups by nature of work	Sex	Housework		Types of time-expenditure Satisfaction of natural physiological needs		Free time	
			min.	%	min.	%	min.	%
1.	Unskilled physical workers	men	174.1	12.2	627.0	43.5	638.9	44.3
		women	294.7	20.4	578.7	40.3	566.6	39.3
2.	Low-grade mental workers	men	152.7	10.6	541.8	37.7	745.5	51.7
		women	284.8	19.9	567.9	39.4	587.3	40.7
3.	Skilled workers (mainly physical) handling machinery	men	144.4	10.0	554.1	38.4	741.5	51.6
		women	191.6	13.3	551.3	33.3	697.1	48.4
4.	Skilled workers doing mainly manual work	men	179.3	12.5	588.2	41.1	672.2	46.4
		women	272.8	18.9	567.8	39.4	599.4	41.7
5.	Highly-skilled workers combining physical and mental work	men	179.2	12.4	566.0	39.4	694.8	48.2
		women	300.0	20.8	549.2	38.2	590.8	41.0
6.	Skilled mental workers	men	142.3	9.9	563.4	39.1	734.3	51.0
		women	304.7	21.2	572.5	39.7	562.8	39.1
7.	Highly-skilled mental workers	men	117.3	8.2	572.6	39.7	750.1	52.1
		women	249.4	17.4	564.7	39.2	625.9	43.4
8.	Supervisors	men	126.7	8.8	566.3	39.4	747.0	51.8
		women	298.8	20.8	553.5	38.4	587.7	40.8

and technical jobs: they spend more time on housework during their day off than they do on other days of the week.

It is interesting, though, that on their day off men in all groups give their wives more help in doing the housework than they do on a full working day or on the shortened working day prior to their day off. This highlights the need for serious explanatory work among the menfolk to involve them more in housework during the week. If they were to help more with housework, it would undoubtedly have a considerable influence on the *de facto* equal rights of men and women in everyday life.

Time spent on satisfying natural physiological needs and free time increase on the day off. Free time takes up over 50 per cent of the entire time budget for some occupational categories, notably for skilled men handling machinery and for men employed on mental jobs. Our attention is also drawn to the wide disparity in free time among women workers in different occupational groups. Thus, while auxiliary working women have only 39.3 per cent of their total time free, shilled women handling machinery enjoy as much as 48.4 per cent of their time free.

Time-budgets related to family status also provide interesting information; we may obtain these by comparing the time-balance of married and single men and women on a working day. Without dwelling on an analysis of working and work-related non-working time, let us note simply that single men and women who work as supervisors do considerably more than the prescribed norm. As a result, men have less free time and women have a substantial cut in time which they would normally spend on satisfying natural physiological needs.

Information on free time and time spent on housework are also very interesting. Among manual workers, as with other occupational grades, single women spend considerably less time on housework than married women; that inevitably gives them a greater share of free time in the overall time-budget structure. Single working women doing highly-skilled mental and physical work actually have more free time than men.

When we consider that the difference in time spent on housework by single and married men is insignificant, we can appreciate again how great the main burden of housework is for the working woman with a family.

At the end of 1967, most Leningrad factories and offices changed over to the five-day week.* That affected time-budgets and led to adjustments in people's everyday lives. The figures obtained at the Kalinin *Skorokhod* factory (see Table XIV) show that working time in all occupational groups began to occupy an average of 33.3 per cent of the 24-hour time-budget. Nonetheless, even in the five-day week, the actual duration of the working day for supervisors of large departments, both men and women, somewhat exceeded the established norm (more than 1.5 hours a week). Time spent on work-associated jobs and on satisfying natural physiological needs has not changed markedly by comparison with the previous survey.

Table XIV
Utilisation of Total Time-Fund on a Working Day, Related to Nature of Work and Sex, 1968

Group by nature of work	Sex	Types of time spent as % of total time-fund					
		Working time	Non-working time connected with work	Housework	Satisfaction of natural physiological needs	Free time	Other time expenditure
1. Unskilled physical workers	men	33.3	4.4	5.0	34.7	21.7	0.9
	women	33.4	4.0	13.0	33.9	14.0	1.7
2. Low-grade mental workers	men	33.3	4.2	7.0	36.1	15.6	3.8
	women	33.4	4.7	13.2	33.3	13.9	1.4
3. Skilled workers (mainly physical) handling machinery	men	33.1	5.3	5.7	34.8	18.5	2.6
	women	33.4	4.9	12.8	35.2	11.3	2.4
4. Skilled workers doing mainly manual work	men	33.3	4.8	5.8	35.5	17.5	3.1
	women	33.5	5.8	13.3	34.4	9.3	3.7
5. Highly-skilled workers combining mental and physical work	men	33.3	5.8	13.3	35.6	10.8	1.2
	women	-	-	-	-	-	-
6. Skilled mental workers	men	33.3	5.8	5.4	36.9	16.2	2.4
	women	33.7	6.4	11.7	37.8	8.2	2.2
7. Highly-skilled scientific and technical personnel	men	-	-	-	-	-	-
	women	33.3	6.9	6.7	34.1	15.4	3.6
8. Supervisors of small departments	men	35.3	4.7	5.9	35.8	14.4	4.2
	women	35.4	6.9	14.4	33.8	8.7	0.8
9. Supervisors of large departments	men	35.4	5.4	5.8	36.0	13.1	4.3
	women	34.7	4.9	13.1	35.4	9.9	2.0

Naturally, our keenest interest in the non-working time-structure is focused on time spent on housework and free time. As in the previous survey, a very considerable amount of time is still being spent on housework during the working day. Women spend an average of three hours a day on housework — *i.e.*, over eleven per cent of their total time-fund. Men spend considerably less (just over an hour in a day). In regard to free time, there seems to be a trend towards less discrepancy in total amount of free time related to sex category, particularly among physical labourers. Under a five-day week, free time makes up 10-20 per cent of the total daily time-budget in all occupational groups.

The time structure on a working day in 1968 was made up as follows: men spent between eight and nine hours each day on satisfying natural physiological needs, 1.0-1.5 hours on travel to work and back, up to 1.5 hours on housework, eight hours on work, and they had up to 4.0-4.5 hours free time. The picture was different for women: they spent only slightly over eight hours a day on satisfying natural physiological needs, 1.0-1.5 hours on non-working time associated with work, over three hours on housework and had an eight-hour working day. They had, at best, some three hours free time.

Free time increased and absolute time spent on housework diminished on the day off after the transfer to the five-day week. (Table XV). By economising on time spent on travel to and from work and cutting down time spent on housework, people are increasing free time to three or four hours a week. Moreover, a certain increase in free time has resulted from changes in the internal structure of the total time-fund and, primarily, from improved conditions which make housework less of a burden.[5] This situation is directly stimulating overall improvements in living standards and the all-round and harmonious development of the personality.

At the same time, we have to note that sex discrepancies are still great. The time women spent on housework in 1968 was quite large (no less than 2.5 hours a day). It is indicative that women engaged on mental work spend more time on housework than working women doing mainly physical work. Evidently, men in all occupational groups do little housework.

The survey showed that the five-day week boosted free time on days off to between seven and ten hours a day. The aggregate time-budget of several grades of workers contains a significant amount of time denoted as 'other time expenditure'. This may well contain reserves of time that could be used as rational free time.

We have only touched upon a few of the questions related to overall time-budget structure and to correlated time-balances of industrial workers and other occupational groups in Leningrad. Nevertheless, they do give us a reasonably full picture of many features of everyday life. We may judge from this material, first, the effect of work-determined social differences on the overall time-budget structure and, secondly, the dismantling of the barriers erected by occupational differences between various urban groups.

Table XV
Utilisation of Non-Working Time on Day Off, Related to Nature of Work and Sex, 1968

Group by nature of work	Sex	Types of time spent as % of total time-fund					
		Working time	Non-working time connected with work	Housework	Satisfaction of natural physiological needs	Free time	Other time expenditure
1. Unskilled physical workers	men	-	-	6.3	39.2	53.4	1.1
	women	-	-	10.4	37.9	41.7	10.1
2. Low-grade mental workers	men	-	-	19.4	42.4	37.5	0.7
	women	0.9	0.1	17.6	37.4	37.7	6.3
3. Skilled workers (mainly physical) handling machinery	men	-	-	5.6	39.1	50.2	5.1
	women	-	-	8.5	37.2	46.4	7.9
4. Skilled workers doing mainly manual work	men	0.5	0.1	4.7	39.4	48.2	7.1
	women	-	-	9.9	38.1	37.8	14.2
5. Highly-skilled workers combining mental and physical work	men	-	-	15.9	41.6	37.7	4.8
	women	-	-	-	-	-	-
6. Skilled mental workers	men	-	-	8.2	40.8	41.0	10.0
	women	0.4	0.7	17.0	43.8	31.0	7.1
7. Highly-skilled scientific and technical personnel	men	-	-	-	47.9	43.0	-
	women	-	-	3.5	-	-	5.6
8. Supervisors of small departments	men	0.5	0.1	6.0	39.2	47.3	6.9
	women	0.1	-	14.3	41.0	38.7	6.1
9. Supervisors of large departments	men	0.5	0.1	8.5	39.3	46.7	4.9
	women	-	-	14.7	39.7	36.2	9.4

The time-budgets give us a reasonably clear idea of material living conditions — a principal element in everyday life. Time spent on housework, for example, indicates people's day-to-day needs and requirements. In turn, material life enables us to spot many factors affecting the formation of family relationships. Moreover, the overall time-budget structure can serve as a basis not only for theoretical judgements on various social aspects of everyday life, but for applied research.

Information on time-utilisation on working and non-working days among workers at the *Skorokhod* factory reveals how the 24 hours is divided up and how each element is related. Naturally, a further increase in free time cannot come in the near future from a drastic cut in the working day. It must come from time related to travel to work and back and, chiefly, from time spent on housework.

The total amount of free time, especially for men, is quite substantial and the immediate problem is evidently not so much to increase it as to use it more rationally.

Let us see how manual workers and other occupational groups in Leningrad disposed of their free time on a working day in 1966 (see Table XVI).

We should stress again that the fact of the time-budget survey being held in summer inevitably affected distribution of free time. Because of summer holidays, many workers were absent or devoted quite a small percentage of time to studying. On the experience of previous surveys of a similar type — that conducted in 1961, for example — it has been established that 18.5 per cent of free time (in a weekly budget) is normally spent on study. [6] In our survey, time devoted to social work was also quite scant, due both to the summer period and to the fact that the survey covered a week rather than a month.

The largest portion of free time went to watching television and listening to the radio. Men, for example, spent an average of 35.4 per cent of their free time every day on viewing TV and listening to the radio. These time expenditures vary greatly among occupational groups. Unskilled male workers spent most time (40.7 per cent) in front of the TV and skilled machine-operators least (25.1 per cent), just ahead of skilled mental workers (27.2 per cent). The other groups showed no sharp fluctuations one way or the other: listening to the radio and watching television took up no less than 32.0 per cent and no more than 35.6 per cent of men's total free-time budget.

Women spent much less time than men watching television and listening to the radio. On the average, these items made up 26.6 per cent of women's total free time. Television enjoyed greatest popularity among unskilled women workers and skilled women doing mainly physical work. We should note, however, that women's time spent viewing TV never fell below 19.7 per cent of their free time.

Among unskilled manual workers, there would appear to be a connection between ownership of a TV set and the amount of time spent on watching television programmes: our survey into domestic furnishings and equipment shows that they had more TV sets than any other group; they also surpassed all other occupational groups in number of TV-viewing hours.

Table XVI
Structure of Free Time of Men and Women on a Working Day, Related to Nature of Work, 1966
(as a percentage of aggregate free time)

Groups by nature of work	Sex	Time with children	Study	Reading socio-political	Reading fiction	Sport	TV and radio	Going to Cinema	Going to Theatre	Parks and Stadiums	Table Games and playing Musical Instruments	Outings without Children	Receiving Guests and visiting Friends and Relations	Work-Hobbies	Inactive Leisure	Other diversions	Other Time Expenditure
1. Unskilled physical workers	men	-	0.9	8.5	10.0	4.5	40.7	6.2	-	6.3	2.9	5.2	0.9	1.0	6.8	1.9	4.2
	women	4.5	0.6	6.0	7.5	0.4	33.7	10.1	-	9.5	0.1	9.0	4.8	0.9	7.8	0.3	4.8
2. Low-grade mental workers	men	-	-	14.0	11.8	-	35.1	2.4	1.2	2.6	2.0	2.7	-	-	9.2	5.8	13.2
	women	5.5	5.8	5.0	9.9	0.5	24.5	10.8	0.6	3.4	0.7	7.9	5.7	4.0	3.5	0.9	11.3
3. Skilled workers (mainly physical) handling machinery	men	4.8	1.0	8.9	9.4	3.3	25.1	8.1	0.3	5.0	2.3	7.6	5.0	3.1	5.7	2.4	8.0
	women	5.1	-	5.4	14.7	2.2	19.7	8.4	1.3	4.3	0.5	4.2	5.1	3.2	15.6	3.1	7.2
4. Skilled workers doing mainly manual work	men	3.6	1.3	9.0	11.1	1.9	33.4	4.8	0.8	5.0	2.7	6.3	2.5	2.1	5.9	2.4	7.2
	women	1.4	-	1.9	7.1	2.5	33.7	6.3	1.4	6.3	0.5	6.3	7.9	0.4	9.3	1.6	13.3
5. Highly skilled workers combining physical and mental work	men	1.0	-	9.8	8.5	0.2	34.2	1.5	-	6.2	7.4	5.7	2.5	1.7	4.2	2.3	14.8
	women	-	-	11.3	12.3	5.7	27.4	1.4	-	6.4	-	8.9	5.3	0.7	3.2	3.3	14.1
6. Skilled mental workers	men	0.6	1.7	12.5	11.0	3.4	27.2	3.0	1.1	4.7	0.6	6.5	2.5	6.1	5.4	2.5	11.1
	women	5.5	-	6.3	10.1	-	25.5	6.4	1.2	3.5	1.1	7.5	9.5	3.7	3.8	2.0	11.9
7. Highly-skilled mental workers	men	3.4	1.7	12.3	10.5	1.4	32.0	4.5	-	0.3	2.4	7.8	4.5	4.2	4.8	0.6	9.6
	women	1.8	4.2	9.4	10.4	1.8	27.4	2.2	-	2.6	-	5.7	6.2	7.2	3.7	3.7	13.7
8. Supervisors	men	0.9	5.2	14.6	9.2	-	35.6	1.7	1.3	1.7	0.2	6.5	3.0	0.6	2.5	5.0	12.0
	women	1.5	2.0	11.7	16.5	0.6	20.8	0.9	10.9	0.9	0.6	6.4	9.8	2.2	2.8	0.8	11.6

Television has evidently become an integral part of the leisure-time of Leningrad workers. Furthermore, by keeping the family home, the television would seem to be a new basis for family solidarity.* Radio and especially television directly affect the reduction in inactive leisure-time, normally filled by conversation, by cutting down the time necessary for people to converse with one another.[7] But, at the same time, these mass media do suggest themes for a great variety of conversations.

In a certain sense we may talk of a type of leisure which is enjoyed 'on the move' (excursions, hikes, etc.). Here we encounter two competing trends: television and open-air rambles. While the former keeps people at home, the latter takes them out into the lap of nature. Through the medium of television the world comes to the individual; during rambles he can comprehend the world through personal experience and his senses.

The huge popularity of television puts a serious responsibility upon TV-planners to ensure that the quality of television programmes should serve the communist education of the public.[8]

Going to the cinema and theatre is a collective form of free time. It comes way behind television and radio in the free-time budget. According to our statistics, manual workers spent more time on visiting the cinema than all categories of mental workers. In turn, the latter, as we see from Table XVI, went to the theatre more often. Cinema-going still accounts for a large amount of free time despite the extensive penetration into everyday life of television.

Reading occupies an important place in the free-time structure. Time spent on reading is more or less the same for all men in our survey. It is interesting that highly-skilled male workers who combine physical and mental work and mental workers invariably devoted more time to socio-political literature than to fiction, while it was just the opposite in the other occupational groups.

Women spent less time than men on reading. It is very noticeable that they came a long way behind men in reading socio-political literature. Thus, skilled working women doing mainly manual work devoted 1.9 per cent of their free time to socio-political literature as against 9.0 per cent for men in the same occupational group. Women supervisors spent more than any other women on reading socio-political literature. It should be emphasised, however, that women in several categories surpassed men in reading fiction (women, for example, in the third and eighth occupational grades).

* It should be borne in mind that one of the chief causes of lack of family solidarity is the husband's drinking. Drunkenness is a serious problem in the USSR and a prime cause of marital strife and breakdown. Thus, a Ukrainian survey shows that as many as 47 per cent of women divorcing their husbands cited drunkenness as the main reason and 63 per cent cited it as an additional reason (see V.S. Zhuchenko, V.S. Steshenko [eds], *Vliyanie sotsial'no-ekonomicheskikh faktorov na demograficheskie protsessy*, Kiev, 1972, p. 128). Television may well be an important contributory factor to keeping the man home and sober.

As with men, a relatively high percentage of women's free time went on visiting parks, gardens and stadiums, and on evenings out. It is indicative that among mental workers there appears to be a reduction in that type of time expenditure. All the same, the statistics show that parks, gardens and other places of mass entertainment should have constant attention as important centres of the public's organised leisure.

Some categories of workers obviously enjoy receiving guests and visiting friends. Almost all occupational groups display a sociability which manifests itself in different ways. During their evenings together people normally act parts at variance with their official position, since social contacts presuppose freedom and a minimum observance of control. People often choose their leisure-partners on a psychological and emotional rather than a formal basis. The chance to choose friends according to one's own interests is very great in the big city today.

Numerical data on areas and types of social contact must be complemented by qualitative indicators within specific situations. It is interesting to trace, for example, the influence of the mass media on conversation-topics in personal contacts. We should also consider the fact that the relationship between the social and psychological realities of functional and non-functional roles may be very delicate and make it extremely difficult to explain genuine mutual relationships.

Our figures may serve as proof that social contact is still a reasonably stable form in which an individual manifests his social needs.

A comparatively small portion of the working-day time-budget (as, too, on the day off and on the shortened day preceding the day off) goes on time with the children; that may be explained by the fact that, in summer, a large number of children leave the town for Young Pioneer camps, recreation bases, country cottages, etc.

As well as elements of free time which help to develop an individual intellectually, there are those that stimulate his physical development, re-create his strength and health. These include sport and all manner of excursions.*

Nowadays people talk long and often about sport. In a certain sense, it is even true to say that sports-conversations are becoming a consolidating force in society. But sport cannot be regarded as being outside the general tenor of life. It has its own traditions in our country and paves the way to understanding aspects of the overall culture in which sports manifest themselves. After the last war, sport grew in importance both here and in many other countries due not only to the popularity of many sports but to psychological factors, like the striving to uphold individual and national vitality, etc.

* Active and regular sport for all is officially regarded as a prerequisite of complete communism in which the new Soviet person would harmoniously "combine spiritual wealth, moral purity and perfect physique" (see "Programme of the Communist Party of the Soviet Union," in *The Road to Communism*, Moscow, 1961, p. 567).

If we look at the figures for time spent on sport and on outings without children, we see at once that active sport still comes low on the list of priorities. In all occupational groups, time spent on sport is less than time spent on outings without the children. Manual workers go in for sport more often and, apparently, on a more regular basis than mental workers. Extensive and painstaking work needs to be undertaken if the share of time spent on sport is to be increased in the total free-time balance. This is all the more important when we consider the objective tendency under socialism towards more mental labour in all economic fields at the expense of physical labour.

The situation in regard to sport is similar in other socialist states. Miklos Santo, who has conducted sociological research in Hungary on this question, has written: "On the one hand, socialist states do extremely well in international sport, sport is extremely popular and many people watch sports events etc. Yet, on the other hand, the results of our survey tell us that mass sport is still not as widespread as it should be . . . "[9] Mass sport has a beneficial effect on both work and leisure, particularly of young people, in so far as it diverts them from wasting their time and, not infrequently, also from misbehaviour and bad habits.

A relatively small amount of time was spent on table games and playing musical instruments. This can only be regretted because the play activity of working people is of paramount importance for normal vitality.[10]

Skilled and highly-skilled scientific and technical workers spent more time than any other group on work-hobbies. Even so, time spent in this way did not rate very highly in the overall free-time fund.

A reasonably high proportion of time went to inactive leisure, so-called undistributed time and 'other' diversions. Manual workers spent more time on passive leisure than all mental groups; on the other hand, mental workers had more undistributed time. Time spent on active leisure usually rises while that spent on passive leisure diminishes. That does not mean people should necessarily do without undistributed time which they may well use very sensibly and rationally (conversing with members of the family, friends, acquaintances, etc.).

Time-expenditure not included in our list probably serves as a source of negative behaviour, consisting of elements that hamper normal development. We refer here to the observance of religious rituals, drunkenness, gambling at cards, etc. While not going into the social causes engendering these negative phenomena, let us state at once that modern man is not a victim of passivity, as for example, Nels Anderson makes him out to be.[11] It is more important to note that the time ascribed to 'passive' leisure does not appear to be a clear-cut trend inherent in a particular occupational group. Of course, this question has to take account of both subjective and objective factors.

The picture changes when we look at time-expenditure on the day off (see Table XVII). Even a brief examination of this table indicates that the proportion of free time spent on listening to the radio, watching television, visiting the cinema or reading books falls sharply on a Sunday in almost all occupational groups. We should stress, however, that in many cases, in absolute figures, time-expenditure on these items is no less on Sunday than on working days. On the day off, people spend considerably more time on going to parks, gardens and stadiums, on outings without the children, receiving guests, visiting friends and relations, doing work-hobbies, engaging in 'other diversions' and other time expenditure not included in the list. They also spend much more time on table games, playing musical instruments and inactive leisure.

Evidently, the principal time-expenditure on days off belongs to leisure and entertainment rather than to raising general educational and cultural standards. The share of free time spent outside the home on Sunday increases in all occupational groups, which stimulates the mounting proportion of time spent on public leisure-activities.

If we differentiate free time by sex, we note that men more often read socio-political literature, spend more time on sport and watching television than women who, in turn, more frequently visit gardens and parks on a Sunday. The figures for free time spent on outings without the children indicate that women mental workers enjoy even more time here than men do. This is apparently due to the fact that men in these intellectual groups devote rather more time to children than do manual working men.

Utilisation of free time is strongly affected by objective and subjective factors (Party affiliation, attitude to studies, participation in socialist competition, etc.). Unfortunately we have no space to make a detailed analysis of these factors. We may note only that, according to our data, **Party** members in all occupational categories spent considerably more time than non-Party members on reading socio-political literature, sometimes at the expense of time spent on reading fiction.

It is interesting that, on a working day, five out of the eight occupational groups show men having almost an identical amount of free time: between 18.0 and 20.6 per cent of the aggregate 24-hour time-budget. These five groups comprise manual workers, low-grade mental workers and skilled mental workers. The amount of free time in the three remaining groups (highly-skilled workers, highly-skilled scientific and technical personnel and supervisors) is also virtually identical, reaching 17.1, 16.2 and 16.0 per cent respectively.

In regard to women, there is also no noticeably sharp discrepancies in total free time. Unskilled manual working women and skilled women operating machinery form the two extremes: their free time comprises 10.0 and 14.2 per cent respectively of the total time-fund. Thus, differences in free-time structure among women are less substantial if we use occupational criteria. Meanwhile, both men and women record a much greater variation in amount of free time on the day off. We have a situation where, as G.V. Osipov and S.F. Frolov[12] rightly point out, people freely choose circumstances which suit their own personalities best.

An examination of the 1968 time-budget study at the *Skorokhod* factory does not reveal any substantial changes on a working day in regard to variety of free

Table XVII
Structure of Free Time of Men and Women on Day Off Related to Nature of Work, 1966
(as a percentage of aggregate free time)

Groups by nature of work	Sex	Time with children	Study	Reading socio-political	Reading fiction	Sport	TV and radio	Going to Cinema	Going to Theatre	Parks and Stadiums	Table Games and playing musical instruments	Outings without children	Receiving Guests and visiting friends and relations	Work-hobbies	Inactive leisure	Other Diversions	Other time-expenditure
1. Unskilled physical workers	men	0.7	0.8	4.5	4.7	0.4	8.5	5.5	2.8	20.9	2.0	14.2	6.2	1.7	8.6	9.3	9.2
	women	4.9	-	1.6	3.4	0.1	14.4	3.5	0.7	18.3	0.5	6.5	10.6	4.5	6.9	9.1	15.0
2. Low-grade mental workers	men	-	-	7.1	4.4	4.6	11.5	0.9	0.9	30.6	1.9	6.4	14.2	-	2.6	1.4	13.5
	women	7.9	1.8	1.8	4.2	2.2	6.9	4.1	-	17.0	0.7	16.8	8.4	2.2	5.0	9.9	11.1
3. Skilled workers (mainly physical) handling machinery	men	3.0	0.5	3.2	3.9	1.1	9.9	3.9	1.5	7.4	1.9	20.9	8.5	6.5	7.8	11.0	9.0
	women	1.8	-	1.3	3.7	-	5.2	4.9	3.0	23.5	-	6.0	10.0	2.0	10.7	12.9	15.0
4. Skilled workers doing mainly manual work	men	2.5	-	3.5	8.2	1.9	16.7	2.6	-	15.9	1.7	6.4	12.9	5.0	6.9	8.5	7.3
	women	3.1	-	1.0	2.8	-	14.2	4.5	3.1	10.9	-	9.3	6.3	1.2	11.2	8.4	24.0
5. Highly-skilled workers combining physical and mental work	men	3.3	-	3.6	3.6	0.1	10.1	0.6	-	20.7	1.8	22.3	4.7	7.5	8.7	5.0	8.0
	women	4.9	0.5	0.5	3.7	-	7.0	2.5	-	30.9	0.5	1.7	9.2	3.6	4.9	10.6	19.5
6. Skilled mental workers	men	1.4	-	3.6	5.6	3.8	6.6	1.8	2.9	7.2	2.0	5.2	13.0	4.8	13.7	18.5	9.9
	women	4.1	-	1.9	7.7	1.6	5.4	2.3	2.5	15.3	-	11.7	13.4	6.8	3.8	11.8	11.7
7. Highly-skilled mental workers	men	3.4	1.4	2.6	10.3	5.2	9.7	1.6	2.1	7.8	1.5	7.4	10.9	6.1	4.6	6.8	18.6
	women	6.0	1.0	3.1	11.1	0.3	5.6	0.9	1.1	8.5	1.7	10.4	10.2	5.5	7.8	13.6	13.2
8. Supervisors	men	3.6	0.6	4.9	4.7	2.0	8.2	1.1	0.4	9.3	1.2	9.2	6.1	11.1	3.5	16.2	17.9
	women	2.5	-	4.4	8.3	5.0	9.8	2.1	0.7	7.3	2.0	13.1	11.5	7.4	6.0	7.1	12.8

time use (see Table XIX). Watching television takes up the greatest amount of free time, as in 1966. Men in all manual occupational grades watch TV for over an hour on average every day — *i.e.*, more than seven hours a week. Women spend at least 40 minutes a day watching television. As we have already pointed out, the proportion of time spent on television falls as we mount the occupational scale. Television is now far more important than such an important channel of mass communication as the radio. Listening to the radio does not exceed 26-28 minutes a day in any occupational group.

Table XIX gives an idea of free-time use on a day off — after the five-day week had been introduced. Yet we do not notice any essential deviation in the free-time structure by comparison with the 1966 material.

The results of our 1966 and 1968 surveys show that the total amount of free time does not sharply vary among the grades studied despite occupational differences that, nonetheless, produce variety in the forms of time-utilisation. At the same time, there are fairly strong variations in free time determined by demographic rather than social factors. It will be a long time before the disproportions between individual urban social groups disappear from the free-time structure representing a function of their objective social status. Summing up, our analysis of free-time budgets testifies to the universal nature of the means of culture and leisure and to equal opportunities for all strata in the urban population to enjoy leisure and recreation. The ways and means by which Leningraders satisfy their cultural tastes are on the whole rational — by which we mean the full and all-round satisfaction by manual workers and other occupational groups of cultural and spiritual needs through expedient use of free time.

Our information enables us to conclude also that Leningrad workers and employees enjoy substantial free time. We agree with V.D. Patrushev that it is hardly right to assert that all occupational groups are currently experiencing insufficient free time.[13] At the same time, we are bound to pose the question of precisely how time should be allocated to socially-necessary, active, creative endeavour and to leisure. According to the results of our time-budget study at the *Skorokhod* factory, for example, leisure-time in all occupational groups was no less than three times more than time spent on socially-necessary creative endeavour and on performing certain family obligations (time spent with children). These figures show that women spent considerably less time than men on social work, studying and improving their qualifications. Yet the gap between men and women in leisure-time is not very great. We are bound to emphasise once again that the total amount of time at the personal disposition of the worker is very high, and on days off it more than doubles, while time for socially-necessary creative endeavour increases much less. This situation reveals once more the exceedingly important role of leisure in contemporary life.

Family and public leisure seem to be developing together: public leisure is at present more popular and, judging by the statistics, many forms of public leisure have much higher prestige than have those of family leisure.

Table XIX
Structure of Free Time of Men and Women on Day Off Related to Nature of Work, 1968

Types of time-expenditure as % of total time-fund

	Groups by nature of work	Sex	Social work	Study and improving qualifications	Time with children	Reading socio-political literature	Reading Fiction	Amateur Art activities	Sport	Listening to radio	Watching Television	Going to cinema	Going to theatre and concerts	Visiting parks, gardens, stadiums, evenings out and mass outings	Playing chess, draughts, dominoes	Receiving guests, visiting friends	Work-hobbies	Inactive leisure and other diversions
1.	Unskilled physical workers	men	-	-	1.4	1.7	6.7	-	3.1	1.7	7.2	3.1	3.1	10.8	2.4	8.5	1.7	2.0
		women	0.1	0.8	1.5	0.8	3.5	-	-	1.4	6.4	1.7	0.3	10.7	0.1	4.2	1.3	8.9
2.	Low-grade mental workers	men	-	-	-	1.3	-	-	-	-	3.5	4.2	5.9	11.3	-	10.4	-	2.2
		women	0.2	0.6	1.7	-	2.7	-	0.6	1.5	6.7	3.3	1.5	5.9	0.1	4.7	3.8	3.2
3.	Skilled workers (mainly physical) handling machinery	men	-	-	1.0	1.3	6.5	-	2.4	1.9	6.3	2.2	0.6	9.9	1.8	4.4	2.2	9.7
		women	0.1	-	3.3	0.8	2.7	0.4	-	0.8	4.9	1.9	1.1	16.6	0.4	4.9	0.4	14.1
4.	Skilled workers doing mainly manual work	men	-	0.1	2.2	1.7	3.1	-	1.8	0.8	6.4	2.6	1.7	15.6	1.1	5.0	1.3	4.8
		women	-	-	0.2	0.4	2.7	-	0.2	0.5	3.6	1.5	0.6	11.7	-	5.5	1.0	9.9
5.	Highly-skilled workers combining physical and mental work	men	-	-	-	0.7	4.2	-	4.9	2.1	4.2	-	2.1	6.5	0.4	9.5	0.8	2.3
		women	-	-	-	-	-	-	-	-	-	-	-	-	-	-	-	-
6.	Skilled mental workers	men	-	-	0.4	2.1	3.4	-	0.1	0.8	6.6	3.1	0.4	11.2	1.6	7.1	2.2	2.0
		women	-	0.2	2.0	0.8	3.3	-	-	0.4	3.8	1.7	0.7	5.5	-	5.9	3.4	3.3
7.	Highly-skilled mental workers	men	-	7.3	-	-	-	-	-	-	8.3	-	-	7.6	-	4.2	15.6	-
		women	-	-	-	-	-	-	-	-	-	-	-	-	-	-	-	-
8.	Supervisors of small departments	men	-	-	1.3	2.3	2.6	-	1.0	1.3	6.6	2.2	0.4	12.8	0.5	8.0	6.9	1.4
		women	-	-	2.7	1.3	4.4	0.4	0.4	0.8	4.7	2.6	1.7	9.3	0.3	6.0	1.3	2.8
9.	Supervisors of large departments	men	-	0.4	3.5	3.3	1.8	-	1.0	1.2	4.0	1.7	1.3	11.7	0.4	3.0	5.5	8.0
		women	-	-	1.5	1.3	2.4	0.3	-	0.3	3.5	1.9	0.3	12.2	0.3	3.6	3.0	5.5

It is also noticeable that there are still many variations in the rational use of free time. Shortcomings stem from objective and subjective elements which are intricately interrelated. On the one hand, the inability of a person or small group to organise leisure is often due to unsatisfactory domestic circumstances, poor organisation of cultural, sporting and other similar institutions, and insufficient free time. On the other hand, it would seem that people often do not exploit opportunities for a progressive way of spending their leisure-time — *i.e.*, subjective factors come into play. The inclination towards a particular form of leisure depends on the environment, whose influence on the individual may be positive or negative. In the latter case, the individual's choice may not only be at odds with society's interests, it may be to the detriment of the individual himself.

In this connection, let us stress that even a simple quantitative increase in free time may occur in various ways. For example, free time may increase faster among mental workers because they enjoy a superior everyday life to people doing mainly physical labour. It is also evident that when there is a reduction in working time (which should come only through economic expediency), the new free time will be utilised variously in different towns and areas of the economy, and among different occupational groups: for some it will augment purely free time, while for others it will go on housework. It will depend not simply on the occupational structure, economic region or residential district, but on many other social and demographic factors. Thus, in the immediate future, actual free time is hardly likely to be synchronous with an increase in time made available by reducing working time or some part of non-working time (travel to and from work, for example) in different towns and social groups.

Our studies have shown that many leisure-forms should be improved to satisfy the growing cultural requirements of the public even in such a big city as Leningrad. This will undoubtedly enable us substantially to alter for the better the balance of free time elements. To do so, we need not only to popularise progressive forms of leisure, but to have a clear idea of public opinion among the various demographic groups in the population. And that, in turn, requires high-level concrete social research that would enable us to understand the meaning of leisure as a source of values, as a means for realising individual creativity and as a basis for the all-round development of the human personality.

2. *Household inventory as a means of studying everyday life*

Our household inventory material enables us to draw conclusions on many aspects of everyday life, especially those which are not open to examination by other methods. Because of their specific nature, household inventory items enable us to judge, at the same time, the material side of everyday life and the cultural standards of the individual or small social group. Such items as TV set, tape recorder and so on may express forms of 'material' and 'spiritual' requirements of the contemporary urbanite. It would be more correct to speak therefore of a 'cultural-everyday life' inventory.

The figures we quote are the first to be published in our country, as far as we know, for 40-odd years.[14] They do not claim to be impeccably accurate, let alone exhaustive. We cannot, of course, use them to draw a complete picture of the standards of culture and everyday life of the occupational groups in our survey. A thorough study of the problem is possible, as stressed earlier, only on the basis of comprehensive research. Nonetheless, we still believe our figures useful in general terms as the results of preliminary exploratory research.

It was not our task to examine the entire inventory; we confined ourselves to a total of seventeen items illustrating the cultural and everyday-life needs of Leningrad engineering workers (in 1965), and to fourteen domestic items, information on which came from research carried out in Tatar towns in 1967. Let us note here that the programmes of these two pieces of research did not envisage any value-judgement on the inventories studied; that, of course, precludes us from drawing any far-reaching conclusions.

The entire inventory may be grouped in the following way, based on the designation of items: furniture (tables — dining and writing, cupboard, settee); items of domestic use (sewing machine); means of transport (motor car, bicycle, motorcycle); electrical appliances (washing machine, refrigerator, vacuum cleaner); cultural items (record player, tape recorder, accordion, piano, radio, television set). This classification has been widely employed by the Budget Statistics Department of the USSR Central Statistical Board.[15]

It is possible to classify the inventory by the extent to which items are used in everyday life. We may therefore subdivide the inventory into the following four groups:

Group I — dining table, wardrobe, settee, bicycle;
Group II — desk, television set, radio, sewing machine, record player;
Group III — washing machine, refrigerator, accordion;
Group IV — motor car, piano (grand piano).

The questionnaire used in the three Tatar towns did not include a question on furniture; so the inventory was classified as follows:

Group I — radio, radio-and-record player, television set, sewing machine;
Group II — camera, washing machine, bicycle and scooter (motorcycle);
Group III — accordion, vacuum cleaner, refrigerator;
Group IV — tape recorder, piano, motor car.

We believe that these inventory groups include items that are typical of everyday urban life and that help to satisfy the useful and rational material and spiritual requirements of Soviet towndwellers. We based ourselves on the hypothesis that distribution of items in such an inventory depends on the occupational status of the family — *i.e.*, it expresses in a general sense the place of the family in the social and economic structure of Soviet society and does not depend on national characteristics, which were given extremely careful consideration in the Tatar study.

In analysing the results, we tried to elucidate the correlation of different items in the various occupational groups. It was important for us to establish whether there existed any tendencies or patterns in the itemised distribution of inventories among different groups. Our general supposition was that inventories vary in a qualitative way among different social strata and that this distinction basically depends on occupational differences, job responsibility, education, per capita income, social origin, etc.

Table XX gives an idea of the relationship between inventory items among occupational groups related to average earnings, average per capita income and size of living space per member of family. The proportion of items in Groups I and II diminishes, and in III and IV rises as we climb the occupational scale. Highly-skilled scientific and technical personnel have the greatest number of items in Groups III and IV, reaching 22.8 per cent in Group III and 6.8 per cent in Group IV — considerably exceeding the average percentage of these items.

It is also noteworthy that low-grade mental workers have virtually the same itemised inventory structure as manual workers without a high occupational status. Highly-skilled workers who combine mental and physical jobs have a similar inventory structure as that of mental workers. Observations of this nature undoubtedly help us to pinpoint common features of everyday life among these occupational groups.

The figures in Table XX are also indicative in that the proportion of furniture in the overall balance diminishes as labour-saving appliances and cultural equipment increase with the growth in earnings, per capita income and average size of living space for each member of the family (though the increase in living space is only slight). This is most apparent with classification by per capita earnings which is, in our view, the best index capable of sensitively registering fluctuations in the extent of distribution and supply of cultural and domestic equipment in the family. As Table XX shows, average earnings of highly-skilled scientific and technical personnel are lower than those of supervisors, yet the average income for each member of the family is higher; this has a marked effect on their inventory structure. Thus, classification by per capita earnings is a more precise way to spotlight differences in the degree of provision of various kinds of inventory than is average earnings.

These data would confirm our assumption that a more or less clear-cut pattern exists of qualitative differences in inventory related to membership of a particular occupational group.

Also in favour of our argument is the material we have showing distribution of inventory-items related to trade and job responsibility. The first thing to note here is the tendency for the share of furniture to diminish with the rise in the occupational index. While dining tables and settees make up 16.9 and 16.7 per cent of the total furniture and equipment of auxiliary manual workers, their share falls to 15.5 and 12.5 per cent of the inventory of flow-line operators (mechanics). The picture is similar in regard to wardrobes. With designers, the ratio is lower than with all other groups.

Distribution of labour-saving devices and cultural equipment is rather different. The share of refrigerators and vacuum cleaners increases in manual worker-families as occupational level rises. The proportion of refrigerators, washing machines and vacuum cleaners in the inventory-balance is much higher for designers than for any other category of worker.

Table XX

Distribution of Itemised Inventory among Leningrad Engineering Workers, 1965*

	Groups by nature of work	Possession of cultural inventory items (%)					Average earnings per person (rub.)	Average earnings (rub.)	Average size of living space per person (sq. m.)
		Group I	Group II	Group III	Group IV	Total			
1.	Unskilled physical workers	44.2	41.7	11.8	2.3	100	60.88	97.52	6.1
2.	Low-grade mental workers	43.3	40.6	13.1	3.0	100	58.45	83.61	6.6
3.	Skilled workers (mainly physical) handling machinery .	43.8	40.6	13.4	2.2	100	64.55	107.55	6.0
4.	Skilled workers doing mainly physical work	41.7	40.0	15.5	2.8	100	62.32	120.00	6.2
5.	Highly-skilled workers combining mental and physical jobs	40.8	38.9	16.7	3.6	100	62.58	129.00	6.4
6.	Skilled mental workers	38.2	37.0	19.1	5.7	100	67.17	109.76	6.8
7.	Highly-skilled scientific and technical personnel	35.9	34.5	22.8	6.8	100	72.24	127.00	6.7
8.	Supervisors	37.3	37.3	19.8	5.6	100	71.12	172.90	6.8
	Total	40.7	39.6	15.7	4.0	100	63.26	113.00	6.3

* (a) The entire sum of cultural and other items in the possession of members of the occupational groups questioned in the survey is taken as 100 per cent.

(b) The survey included only personal inventory-items belonging to the family or a single person, and not those belonging to hostels and used by families or single persons renting part of a room, etc.

If we turn to cultural equipment, we see that here, too, its share mounts as we move up the occupational scale. This is especially marked with record players and tape recorders. Accordions, on the other hand, are to be found more with auxiliary manual workers: 2.3 per cent of the inventory of auxiliary manual workers and only one per cent of workers who combine mental and physical labour. Naturally, the provision of musical instruments in the family often depends on the personal inclination of its members. There does appear to be, however, a connection between listening to the radio and possession of records and tapes. The more people listen to the radio, the more often they possess their own musical instrument. In this respect, too, there is a particularly high correlation among people who have many records and tapes.

We may note one rather curious detail in distribution of one item of household equipment: more TV sets among unskilled workers than among other Leningrad engineering workers. This bears out the contention that the television has become an integral part of everyday life of manual workers and other groups in Leningrad. We should point out once again that the television tends to unite the family because its members often watch one and the same programme which they discuss among themselves. All the same, we should take cognisance of the fact that this family unity is of an individual character and is directly dependent upon the size of the family and differences in the age of parents and children.

Motor cars and pianos are not very widespread. Thus, of the 274 metal-cutting lathe operators, only six have a car — *i.e.*, a little over two cars for every hundred workers in this category. In the overall inventory balance, cars come highest with designers — 1.7 per cent by comparison with 0.8 per cent with highly-skilled workers combining mental and physical work. Among the other groups, the share of cars is even lower. However, nearly all groups surpassed designers in share of bicycles and motorcycles.

On the whole, the motor car, which is important to family unity, is popular in the occupational groups in our study, in spite of its modest place in the overall inventory of all categories of workers.[16] The 24th Party Congress Ninth Five-Year Plan Directives for 1971-75 provide for an almost four-fold increase in car production.[17] So the motor car is today, and even more so in the near future, becoming more and more part of everyday life.

If we take job-responsibility as our indicator, we can compare inventory distribution within families of manual workers, team-leaders and assistant foremen, foremen and other Leningrad engineering grades. The proportion of such items as dining table, wardrobe and settee is higher with manual workers than it is with foremen and supervisors. On the other hand, the latter show a higher percentage of labour-saving appliances and cultural equipment. Meanwhile, we should add that here, too, there are certain discrepancies. For example, there is almost no difference in distribution of desks among all the groups studied. Once again we find that manual workers have 2.8 per cent more televisions than supervisors of workshops, departments, bureaux and laboratories. The latter, however, invariably have a higher percentage of refrigerators, washing machines, vacuum cleaners, tape recorders and record players over all other groups.

The figures showing distribution of items relating to education levels reveal a reasonably clear tendency for the share of labour-saving appliances and cultural equipment to increase in step with education level, which is also closely connected with vocational training. True, in this instance, too, the percentage of TV sets among people with low education is higher than it is among persons with complete secondary specialised, incomplete higher or higher education.

Sewing machines, which make up a major item in the overall inventory balance, do not seem to set any pattern in distribution among the various groups. A high percentage of sewing machines would indicate that certain items of dress are made at home, a situation that is probably common to manual worker and other social groups alike. But the significance of sewing machines in the inventory of manual workers is today much more modest than it was during the 1920's when there was one machine for every two worker-families.[18]

We have devoted considerable attention to itemised inventories and have tried to test the proposition that a tendency exists towards distribution of items related to occupation. To test this further, it is useful to look at statistics on household items for every 100 Leningrad engineering workers related to cash earnings per member of the family (see Table XXI).

The value of Table XXI is that it gives us a visual picture both of overall provision of domestic equipment and of distribution related to per capita earnings.

We have made a survey only of personal furniture and equipment. In Leningrad, as in many other Soviet cities, availability of technical equipment depends not only on per capita income but on equipment-hiring bases. Leningrad, in fact, is one of the top cities in the country in provision of such bases and that, of course, in some way improves the situation, giving families more domestic appliances and other equipment.

In the last few years, household inventories have seen drastic changes. New flats are normally fitted out with modern furniture ensuring comfort, beauty and hygiene and this has a direct effect on the improving culture of everyday urban life.

On the subject of the relatively well-furnished homes of manual workers, we should note that total furniture is more or less stable for every 100 persons with an income of between 30 and 70 rubles per family member, but it falls sharply for those in the 20-30 ruble income range. The number of items of furniture is also less in the 70-100 rubles per capita income group, but this is due to more labour-saving devices and cultural items.

The amount of labour-saving devices tends to increase with a rise in per capita income of 20-30 rubles have 5.7 washing machines, 2.3 refrigerators and 14.8 vacuum cleaners per 100 persons, while families in the 70-100 ruble bracket have 12.3, 20.4 and 19.8 items respectively. Yet certain discrepancies exist here too. As one example, families in the 50-60 ruble range have rather fewer washing machines than have those with 30-50 rubles. The lowest income groups have

Table XXI

Number of Inventory-Items per 100 Persons, Related to Per Capita Earnings of Leningrad Engineering Workers, 1965.

Average monthly cash earnings per member of the family (rubles)	Number of items of cultural and domestic use per 100 persons													
	Dining table	Desk	Wardrobe	Settee	Washing machine	TV set	Refrigerator	Radio	Bicycle	Scooter (motor-bike)	Sewing machine	Vacuum cleaner	Record player	Tape recorder	Accordion	Piano (grand piano)
20 – 30	78.3	23.8	69.2	64.9	5.70	92.0	2.3	30.1	23.8	9.10	55.7	14.80	18.0	0.00	5.57	2.28
30 – 40	95.0	42.5	92.2	83.1	7.46	70.5	10.0	47.0	20.0	4.85	62.7	6.34	22.8	5.23	8.95	2.24
40 – 50	97.2	45.2	93.1	83.5	8.46	67.0	9.76	49.2	23.5	4.88	58.7	11.05	22.9	3.38	5.63	4.70
50 – 60	93.0	41.5	91.8	82.0	6.98	69.8	12.0	51.0	19.3	5.63	55.7	9.30	27.8	6.50	7.45	3.50
60 – 70	92.0	44.7	91.3	84.4	10.75	66.0	16.1	52.8	19.0	5.00	58.2	12.45	27.8	8.90	8.10	5.90
70 – 100	88.4	46.0	87.2	78.7	12.30	68.0	20.4	57.5	21.0	5.33	54.5	19.80	33.6	12.30	8.25	5.80

more than twice as many vacuum cleaners as the next group (30-40 rubles). On the whole, however, these discrepancies do not alter the overall pattern in distribution of domestic machines and appliances related to average income per member of the family.

Provision of televisions, bicycles and motorbikes presents rather a unique picture in that they tend to be more in the possession of families with the lowest per capita income. While families in the 20-30 rubles range have 92 TV sets, 23.8 bicycles and 9.1 motorbikes per 100 persons, families in the 70-100 rubles bracket have, respectively, 68, 21 and 5.3. As we see, the discrepancy in distribution of TV sets is particularly noticeable. In that connection, we would stress once again that not only social conditions determine a family's specific choice of domestic equipment, people themselves select, from the wide variety of furniture and equipment available, the items which most conform to their personal inclinations. It would be wrong to rely only on the 'bare bones' of the household item-distribution and occupational structure, even though it is of paramount importance. It is imperative to treat everyday life as an individual as well as a social phenomenon.

Information on distribution of domestic goods related to size of family does not show any distinct trends and patterns. Evidently, the family-size alone cannot serve as a criterion of item-distribution without account for the number of persons working and the per capita family earnings. In addition, distribution of domestic items is also influenced by social origin. Examination of data on item-distribution related to social origin of the mother when the person in the survey starts work reveals a tendency towards an increasing share of desks, washing machines, refrigerators, vacuum cleaners, record players and tape recorders among women employees by comparison with working women, collective-farm women and women working a home-farm singlehanded. The situation is similar in regard to social origin according to the father. But we were unable to establish any pattern in distribution of the remaining domestic items related to social origins of the parents.

In his work *Domestic Everyday Life According to Inventories,* S.G. Strumilin gives prominence to research into household inventories among Leningrad manual workers . We can therefore make some general comparisons. First, it would seem that "cultural poverty and archaic habits in the worker's material environment" are things of the past.[19] Secondly, present-day cultural and domestic equipment is considerably richer both in regard to furniture and to new, hitherto unknown labour-saving devices and cultural equipment. This circumstance, in addition to the massive rehousing of worker-families into new well-appointed flats, is making a fundamental contribution to the radical reconstruction of the worker's everyday life. Thirdly, disparities in home environment between manual workers and other urban social groups are being more rapidly overcome today than they were in the 1920's. The CPSU Party Programme and other Party documents stress that as society develops, differences in material and cultural standards will diminish, so causing a continual erosion of social distinctions.

Comparative material on Leningrad engineering workers in 1965 and 1970 indicate above all the quantitative growth in labour-saving devices and cultural equipment in all occupational groups without exception. Obviously, improving welfare has much to do with this. Thus, the number of refrigerators and washing machines increased by 6.0-11.0 per cent among worker-families over the five-year span. There was also an increase in TV sets (by 2.0-5.0 per cent) and tape recorders (5.0-8.0 per cent).

Of particular interest is the relationship between inventories and occupational groups in 1970. In order of provision, first place goes to TV sets and radios followed by sewing machines, refrigerators, washing machines, vacuum cleaners and tape recorders in all categories. At the same time, mental workers outstrip manual workers in provision of electrical appliances and cultural items. Thus, unskilled manual workers have virtually half as many refrigerators as have the families of designers. But TV sets, as before, tend to predominate in the families of manual workers.

In making a general evaluation of the household inventory, we must once again make the point that there are obviously insufficient home appliances (refrigerators, washing machines, vacuum cleaners, etc.) to fill up the gaps in the still inadequate Leningrad communal services such as canteens and cafes, laundries, ready-cooked meals shops, etc. This conclusion is confirmed by other Leningrad surveys.[20]

This inadequate provision of domestic appliances is adversely affecting the growth in free time, particularly among working women with young children. This is a conclusion we made, too, when studying the time-budgets of manual workers and other social groups in Leningrad. G.S. Petrosyan makes the relevant point that use of a washing machine can reduce housework-time from 24.3 to 21.3 per cent (of total free time) and, with a refrigerator, floor polisher and vacuum cleaner, even to 20.7 per cent.[21]

Let us now turn to data from the three Tatar towns mentioned above. Examination of the data enable us to establish the following patterns in distribution of domestic items related to education — which shows a high correlation with occupational structure (see Table XXII).

The first point to note is the reduction in Group I items and an increase in items of Groups III and IV as education and occupational status rise in all three towns; discrepancies are extremely small. For example while the share of Group I items among persons who have four-six classes of education comprises 56.2, 51.1 and 51.9 per cent in Kazan, Almetyevsk and Menzelinsk respectively, their share falls correspondingly to 32.8, 35.6 and 38.0 per cent in the three towns among people who have a higher education. The opposite situation obtains in distribution of items in Groups III and IV in the three towns: tape recorders, pianos and motor cars make up 3.1, 2.9 and 2.1 per cent among people with four-six classes as against 12.3, 11.0 and 7.0 per cent respectively among people with higher education living in the same towns.

Meanwhile, Group II items are distributed more or less evenly, irrespective of education or occupational group. We assume that this situation is due to the fact that these items have already reached complete saturation point or, at least, if not qualitatively, they are extensively available to urban families.

All three towns and all occupational groups show a progressive reduction in domestic items from Groups I to IV in the total balance. The proportion of items in Groups III and IV is several times less than in Group II, even more so than Group I. This underlines the fact that consumer goods in these groups, despite their fairly wide distribution, still occupy a modest place in item-selection in our survey. That evidently is attributable to the short supply of some of these commodities and the low prestige of others among certain social strata and urban groups. Material living standards, of course, affect the provision of several inventory-items. Far from every family, for example, is able to buy a new car.

We have to remember that the material requirements of social groups are changing rapidly in modern urbanised society and production does not always satisfy the demand in time. An imbalance between mounting material needs and available supply has an adverse effect on a person's work as well as his behaviour at home. Nevertheless, the items we examined do testify to the growing individualisation' in the town, expressed in a preference for certain items rather than others. There can be no doubt that cultural and domestic equipment will never be a uniform pattern both because of socio-political relations and because of the strong effect of socio-psychological factors on this process.

Before we commenced our research in Tataria, we obtained information on preliminary interviews taken from some of the people in the sample. From this we were able to examine the influence of national characteristics on distribution of household inventory-items among urban groups and to formulate our present hypothesis. The concrete data to which we now refer confirm the absence of any stable link between distribution of domestic items and national characteristics in all three towns. For example, the proportion of Group I items among Russians in Kazan and Menzelinsk was 46.6 and 47.4 per cent, while among Tatars it was 47.5 and 46.9 per cent respectively. A similar consistent pattern, though not so clear-cut, may be traced with items in the three other groups. Typically, the Chuprov coefficients completely bear out our conclusions.

Data on cultural and domestic equipment indicate that material living standards are continually rising and that household inventories may symbolise the social status of an individual or social group. Our opinion on this issue is shared by the authors of one of the first works written on this theme.[22] It is also apparent that the possession of household items, despite their universality and simplicity, requires account for the socio-psychological factors that greatly affect the formation of the basis of material everyday life in Soviet towns. This emphasises once more the complexity of the processes of everyday life which, although determined by the sphere of production, are not rigidly tied to it.e

Table XXII

Distribution of Household Inventory-Items among Urban Families in the Tatar Autonomous Republic, 1967.

Education	Cultural and domestic equipment inventory (%)												
	Group I			Group II			Group III			Group IV		
	Kazan	Almet-yevsk	Menzel-insk	Kazan	Almet-yevsk	Menzel-insk	Kazan	Almet-yevsk	Menzel-insk	Kazan	Almet-yevsk	Menzel-insk
Up to four classes	63.0	54.9	33.9	18.3	29.7	26.3	7.3	7.7	2.6	2.4	2.6	1.3
4-6 classes	56.2	51.1	51.9	22.0	30.0	35.5	12.0	13.2	3.9	3.1	2.9	2.1
7-9 classes	51.6	46.0	47.1	23.8	30.6	34.0	13.0	10.6	7.7	4.0	3.3	2.3
10-11 classes	45.2	40.5	45.9	25.5	29.7	33.0	14.4	16.7	10.1	5.9	5.1	3.2
Tekhnikum	42.1	33.0	46.9	24.8	29.1	35.7	21.1	20.0	9.2	6.9	7.7	3.1
Incomplete higher	37.9	37.8	38.0	25.1	30.8	34.0	20.0	18.0	16.0	6.0	8.1	8.0
Higher	32.8	35.6	38.0	26.4	27.1	31.0	25.4	25.3	16.3	12.3	11.0	7.0

The concrete material on which we have relied confirms our above-stated hypothesis that belonging to a certain milieu leaves its imprint on the quantity and quality of a household inventory. We are aware that the facts we have adduced have left untouched a large number of other questions associated with the household inventory. This problem is far from being uni-dimensional. It requires the further accumulation of facts, their examination and testing in subsequent concrete investigations by representatives of many sciences — economists, statisticians, historians, sociologists, etc. Our conclusions are by no means final; they are merely a step towards unraveling the problem.

At the present time, the situation is made complex by the fact that household inventory studies are insufficiently illuminated by programmes of the state statistical agencies. Therefore, we do not have at our disposal anywhere near full data of a nationwide character or other more or less regular surveys of household inventories, carried out in other Soviet towns, which we might use for comparative purposes.

Conclusions

We have looked at everyday life as a sphere of social life reflecting the day-to-day and, at the same time, the historical ways in which people satisfy their material and cultural requirements. Everyday life depends on the economic development of society and cannot be static; it changes together with technical, economic and social progress.

As a phenomenon of non-productive life, with the laws immanent in it, everyday life exerts a reverse effect on production, accelerating technical progress and thereby helping to increase the cultural and technical standards of manual workers, technical and engineering personnel and employees. In the sum total of socio-economic relations, everyday life is bound up with the occupational structure of society at a given stage of its development and with socio-pyschological factors inherent in a person, a class, social group, etc. Being determined by social relations and social structure, everyday life acts as their attribute.

Therefore, we can only approach such a complicated and multi-faceted phenomenon of social reality as everyday life by strictly observing the principle of unity of theoretical and empirical approaches, methodology and methods.

In so far as socialism does not appear in a ready-made form, but emerges from the womb of capitalism, socialist society will long retain a certain inequality with its own objective basis. In productive life, this inequality springs from the nature of specific labour, the extent of its division into skilled and unskilled work, and other factors. The existence of discrepancies in production leads, naturally, to inequality in distribution of the gross social product and its consumption; hence the need to study everyday life with account for occupational structure.

The present research is, to a considerable extent, of a local nature because of the limited number of areas where the concrete social surveys were conducted. But the results do enable us to make the following conclusions:

1. There still remain differences in everyday life due to the occupational division of the urban population.

2. A marked trend is discernible towards a 'smoothing out' of disparities in the everyday life of towndwellers. As previous experience would indicate, the everyday-life model in socialist and communist society will increasingly reflect its unification through the gradual material and cultural convergence of the different social strata and groups in the urban population; that is a paramount condition for the successful construction of communism.

3. We noted a particularly distinct tendency towards a mitigation of differences through the informal structure and, primarily, within the family, which acts as an integrating cell in mollifying discrepancies in occupation and everyday life.

Our concrete material on the everyday life of manual workers, technical and engineering personnel and employees provides ample evidence of rising living standards. This is particularly apparent in regard to housing: millions of urban families are annually improving their housing conditions. It is also welcome to note the high level of consumption of foodstuffs and consumer durables which, in quantitative terms, is ensuring that all Soviet towndwellers do not lack material comforts. The main target now in regard to the material welfare of urban, as of all Soviet people, is to improve the consumption-structure of foodstuffs and the supply of consumer durables, to reach scientifically-established standards.

Major changes are taking place in the structure of the urban family. The nature of family relations reveals a process, common and natural for Soviet life, that is producing a uniform type of family and a uniform structure of everyday life; moreover, both these basic units are in dialectical unity. It should be emphasised, however, that although a working woman with young children enjoys equal economic, political and legal rights with the man, she continues to be at a disadvantage in regard to everyday life, simply because she has to bear the brunt of the burden in the home and in looking after young children. We must once again draw attention to the immense concern being shown by the Party and Soviet government in improving housing construction, health protection and consumer services.[1]

Their Leninist approach to cultural tasks has enabled the CPSU substantially to improve the cultural standards of Soviet towndwellers and, above all, of the working class. Lenin once made it plain that what "we need is a vast increase in culture."[2]

The problem of free time is today acute. L.I. Brezhnev, General Secretary of the CPSU Central Committee, had this to say on the issue at the Fifteenth USSR Trade Union Congress: "Free time may be regarded as truly public wealth only when it is utilised for people's all-round development, for developing their talents and, thereby, for expanding the material and cultural potential of society even more. Socialism has created the conditions necessary for this, has granted Soviet people sufficient free time for relaxation, for improving their education and culture, fortifying their health and physical development, bringing up their children and for other useful matters."[3] It follows that a further study of free time has prime importance and interest for the practical activity of Party, state and public organisations. This is particularly worth noting because considerable deficiencies do exist in the organisation of leisure, for objective and subjective reasons. Much has still to be done to improve the various forms of leisure.

Our research enables us once again to perceive quite clearly that the unity of urban social groups is being cemented on a single ideological and political basis. Furthermore, people are increasingly becoming unified in their everyday life because discrepancies among different social groups are visibly diminishing. We should here bear in mind the point made by L.I. Brezhnev that "The convergence of all classes and social groups, the inculcation of moral and political qualities in the Soviet people and the strengthening of their social unity are all occuring on the foundation of Marxist-Leninist ideology which expresses the socialist interests and communist ideals of the working class."[4]

This work, as we have emphasised, has left unanswered many questions concerning urban life, largely because a thorough sociological and historical study of everyday life is a comparatively new area. More experience has to be accumulated. This is a problem that will require the concerted efforts of representatives of many social disciplines, the further gathering of information, its systematic analysis and logical synthesis.

Notes

Introduction

1   *SSSR i zarubezhnye strany posle Velikoi Oktyabr'skoi sotsialisticheskoi revolyutsii. Stat. sb.*, Moscow, 1970, p. 24.
2   *Materialy XXIV s'yezda KPSS,* Moscow, 1971, p. 137.
3   See A.V. Ikonnikov, *Sotsiologicheskie predposylki razvitiya sovetskovo gradostroitel'stva,* Moscow, 1970; M.L. Strongina,*Sotsial'no-ekonomicheskie problemy razvitiya bol'shikh gorodov v SSSR,* Moscow, 1970, etc.

Chapter 1   Methodological and Methodical Principles of Urban Research in the USSR

1   See V.G. Sinitsyn, *Sovetsky obraz zhizni,* Moscow, 1969; S.G. Spasibenko, *Byt – sostavnaya chast' sotsialisticheskovo obraza zhizni.* Uch. zap. MGPI im. V.I. Lenina, vyp. 348, Part II, Moscow, 1970.
2   L.A. Anokhina, V.Yu. Krupyanskaya, M.N. Shmeleva, "Byt i yevo preobrazovaniya v period postroyeniya sotsializma," *Sovetskaya etnografiya,* No. 4, 1965, p.16.
3   *Filosofskaya entsiklopediya,* Vol. 1, Moscow, 1960 p.206.
4   A.G. Kharchev, "Byt i sem'ya pri sotsializme," *Voprosy filosofii,* No. 3, 1967. Somewhat later, Kharchev began to interpret the concept 'everyday life' differently. In his present opinion, the term can only be used to designate the sphere of services to and for oneself (see A.G. Kharchev, *Byt i sem'ya v sotsialisticheskom obshchestve,* Leningrad, 1968, p.5). In our view this standpoint is entirely wrong.
5   V. Sinitsyn, *Byt epokhi stroitel'stva kommunizma. (O putyakh stroitel'stva kommunisticheskovo byta v SSSR),* Chelyabinsk, 1960, p.13.
6   B.D. Parygin, *Sotsial'naya psikhologiya kak nauka,* Leningrad, 1965, pp. 175-176.
7   It is patently apparent that a mechanical application of concepts from one

discipline to another does not help to elucidate many important questions if only because even mixed disciplines approach the same phenomena in different ways. Thus, for example, when an ethnographer studies eating habits, he focuses his attention on the nature of the food, the dietary habits of different peoples, while a sociologist, economist or historian is interested in so-called economic consumption; moreover, the methods will not coincide: While an ethnographer will try to obtain information primarily from direct observation, a sociologist will base himself on budgetary data gathered by state statistical agencies or by researchers interested in obtaining that type of material to determine the amount and calory-value of the products consumed. We are objecting only to unwarranted transfer of concepts from one discipline to another, and not to the actual use of the data of one discipline by another.

8 *Kommunist*, No. 8, 1967, p.65.
9 G.V. Osipov, S.F. Frolov, "Vnerabocheye vremya i yevo ispol'zovanie," in *Sotsiologiya v SSSR*, Vol. 2, Moscow, 1966, pp. 235-236.
10 See K. Marx i F. Engels, *Works* (in Russian), Vol. 23, pp. 668-685.
11 *Ibid.*, Vols. 2 and 18.
12 V.I. Lenin, *Collected Works* (Russian), Vol. 3, p. 143.
13 On this question see, for example, V.D. Patrushev,*O nekotorykh voprosakh vyborki v sotsiologicheskikh obsledovaniyakh. Nauchny seminar po primeneniyu kolichestvennykh metodov v sotsiologii*, vyp. 2, Novosibirsk, 1966.
14 G.S. Petrosyan, *Vnerabocheye vremya trudyashchikhsya v SSSR*, Moscow, 1965, p. 47.
15 See G.A. Prudensky: 1. "Voprosy uchyota vnerabochevo vremeni," *Voprosy ekonomiki*, No. 4, 1959; 2. "Svobodnoye vremya trudyashchikhsya v sotsialisticheskom obshchestve," *Kommunist*, No. 15, 1960; 3. "Izuchenie byudzhetov vremeni (voprosy struktury i klassifikatsii)," *Voprosy ekonomiki*, No. 1, 1967, and other works by him.
16 See, for example, *Recherche comparative internationale sur les budget temps. VIe Congres mondial de sociologie*, 4 – 11 September, 1966, Evian.
17 P.P. Maslov, *Sotsiologiya i statistika*, Moscow, 1967.
18 *Ibid.*, p. 226.
19 See L.A. Gordon, V.Ya. Volk et al. 1. "Nekotorye problemy tipologii svobodnovo vremeni," *Informatsionny byulleten' SSA*, No. 24, 1969; 2. "Tipologiya slozhnykh sotsial'nykh yavleniy," *Voprosy filosofii*, No. 7, 1969.
20 B. Grushin, *Svobodnoye vremya. Aktual'nye problemy*, Moscow, 1967, p. 15.
21 V.A. Artemov, V.I. Bolgov et al., *Statistika byudzhetov vremeni trudyashchikhsya*, Moscow, 1967.
22 Grushin, *op. cit.*, p. 14.
23 See, for example, B.D. Parygin, *Sotsial'naya psikhologiya kak nauka*, Leningrad, 1967, p. 196.

24 This view is shared by other authors: see V.I. Bolgov, "Kategoriya vremeni v sotsial'nom izmerenii i planirovanii i problema ekonomii vremeni," *Sotsial'nye issledovaniya. Problemy byudzheta vremeni trudyashchikhsya*, vyp. 6, Moscow, 1970, pp. 59-60.
25 See K. Marx i F. Engels, *Works* (Russian), Vol. 46, Part II, p. 221.
26 G.V. Osipov, S.F. Frolov, (*op. cit.*, p.228) take the opposite view.
27 See, for example, A.W. Green, *Recreation, Leisure and Politics,* New York, 1964, p. 59.
28 M. Kaplan, *Leisure in America: A Social Inquiry,* New York, 1960, p. 22.
29 M.N. Neumeyer and E.S. Neumeyer, *Leisure and Recreation. A Study of Leisure and Recreation in their Sociological Aspects,* New York, 1958; E. Larrabee and R. Meyersohn (eds.) *Mass Leisure,* Glencoe, Ill., 1958, M.E. Mulack, *Leisure – Time for Living and Retirement,* New York, 1961; D. Hanhart, *Arbeiter in der Freizeit. Eine sozialpsychologische Untersuchung.* Berne-Stuttgart, 1964; J.B. Nash, *Recreation: Pertinent Readings – Guide Posts to the Future,* Dubuque, Iowa, 1965.
30 See A.G. Kharchev, M.N. Perfiliev, "Dosug molodyozhi i yevo problemy," *Sotsial'nye issledovaniya,* vyp. 2, Moscow, 1968.
31 See A.W. Green, *op. cit.,* p. 50.
32 See, for example, H. Swados, "Less Work – Less Leisure," in E. Larrabee and R. Meyersohn (eds.), *Mass Leisure,* Glencoe, III, 1960, p. 359.
33 G. Ye Zbrovsky, G.P. Orlov, *Dosug: deistvitel'nost i illyuzii. Problema svobodnovo vremeni v marksistskoi i burzhuaznoi sotsiologii,* Sverdlovsk, 1970.

Chapter 2   **From the History of Urban Studies in the USSR and Abroad**

1 See, for example, S. Prokopovich, "Byudzhety peterburgskikh rabochikh," *Zapiski Russkovo tekhnicheskovo obshchestva,* XLIII, Nos. 2, 3, 4, 1909; M. Dapidovich, *Byudzhety peterburgskikh tekstil'nykh rabochikh,* St. Petersburg, 1912; A.M. Stopani, *Neftepromyshlenny rabochiy i yevo byudzhet,* Second edition, Moscow, 1924, etc.
2 For greater detail, see V. Yu. Krupyanskaya, *Voprosy etnograficheskovo izucheniya byta rabochikh. Etnograficheskoye izuchenie byta rabochikh. Po materialam otdel'nykh promyshlennykh raionov SSSR,* Moscow, 1968, pp. 7-10; L.A. Anokhina, M.N. Shmeleva, "Nekotorye problemy etnograficheskovo izucheniya sovremennovo russkovo goroda," *Sovetskaya etnografiya,* No. 5, 1964, p. 9.
3 S.G. Strumilin, *Problemy ekonomiki truda,* Moscow, 1957, p. 209. (Here and subsequently we cite the later edition of Academician Strumilin's works.)
4 *Ibid.,* p. 210.
5 *Ibid.*

6   This theme is reflected in the works of other writers. See, for example, G.S. Pollyak, *Byudzhety rabochikh i sluzhashchikh k nachalu 1923 goda,* Moscow, 1924; V. Il'insky, *Byudzhet rabochikh SSSR v 1922-1926,* Moscow, 1928.
7   S.G. Strumilin. 1. *Domashniy byt po inventaryam. Problemy ekonomiki truda;* 2. *Rabochiy byt v tsifrakh. Statistika ekonomichekie etyudy,* Moscow-Leningrad, 1926.
8   S.G. Strumilin, *Problemy sotsializma i kommunizma v SSSR,* Moscow, 1962, pp. 375-378.
9   Ye. Kabo, *Pitanie russkovo rabochevo do i posle voiny (po statisticheskim materialam 1908-1924 gg.),* Moscow, 1926.
10 *Ibid,* p. 95.
11 *Ibid,* p. 127.
12 See E. Engel, *Die Lebenkosten belgischer Arbeiterfamilien fruher und jetzt,* Dresden, 1895.
13 Ye. O. Kabo, *Ocherki rabochevo byta (opyt monograficheskovo issledovaniya domashnevo byta),* Vol. I, Moscow, 1928.
14 *Ibid.,* p. 21.
15 P. Berezin et al., *Rabochaya molodyozh', kak ona yest'. Opyt nauchno-pedagogicheskovo izucheniya molodyozhi odnovo zavoda,* Priboi, Leningrad, 1930.
16 S. Lapitskaya, *Byt rabochikh Tryokhgornoi manufaktury,* Moscow, 1935.
17 See M.N. Lyadov, *Voprosy byta,* Moscow, 1925; M. Rafail, *Za novovo cheloveka,* Leningrad, 1928; D. Lebedev, *Golos millionov (opyt obsledovaniya 16,000 pisem rabochikh korrespondentov),* Moscow-Leningrad, 1928; I. Zhiga, *Novye rabochie,* Second edition, Moscow-Leningrad, 1928, etc.
18 See *Byudshety leningradskikh rabochikh i sluzhashchikh v 1922-1926 gg.,* Moscow, 1929; *Trud v SSSR. Spravochnik. 1926-1930,* Moscow, 1930. *Trud i profdvizhenie v Leningradskoi oblasti. Stat. spravochnik,* Moscow, 1932; *XV let diktatury proletariata (ekonomiko-statisticheskiy sbornik po g. Leningradu i Leningradskoi oblasti),* Leningrad, 1932, etc.
19 M. Krivitsky, "K voprosu o metodologii izucheniya urovnya zhizni rabochikh," *Problemy ekonomiki,* No. 2, 1935; S. Heinman, "Uroven' zhizni trudyashchikhsya SSSR," *Planovoye khozyaistvo,* No. 8, 1936.
20 S.G. Strumilin, *Problemy ekonomiki truda,* Moscow, 1957. This work first appeared in the journal *Planovoye khozyaistvo,* No. 7, 1925, and is a continuation of one of his earlier pieces of research on the theme "Byudzhet vremeni russkovo rabochevo v 1922 g.," *Voprosy truda,* Nos. 3-4, 1923.
21 S.G. Strumilin, *Problemy ekonomiki truda,* p. 269.
22 V. Mikheyev, *Byudzhet vremeni rabochikh i sluzhashchikh Moskvy i Moskovskoi oblasti,* Moscow-Leningrad, 1932.
23 V. Lebedev-Patreiko, G. Ravinovich and D. Rodin, *Byudzhet vremeni rabochei sem'i (po materialam leningradskovo obsledovaniya),* Leningrad, 1933.

24 Several valuable data are to be found on time-budgets in a number of the above-mentioned statistical handbooks. See, for example, *Trud v SSSR. Ekonomiko-statisticheskiy spravochnik,* Moscow, 1932, pp. 169-176; *Trud i profdvizhenie v Leningradskoi oblasti. Stat. spravochnik,* Leningrad, 1932, pp. 98-101.

25 S.P. Partigul, *Statistika material'novo i kul'turnovo urovnya naroda,* Moscow, 1956; S.P. Figurnov,*Real'naya zarabotnaya plata i pod'yom material'novo blagosostoyaniya trudyashchikhaya v SSSR,* Moscow, 1960; R.S. nazarov, V.M. Sinyutin, Yu. L. Shirlin, *Potreblenie v SSSR i metodika yevo ischisleniya,* Moscow, 1959; *Metodologicheskie voprosy izucheniya urovnya zhizni trudyashchikhsya,* Moscow, 1959; "Voprosy povysheniya urovnya zhizni trudyashchikhsya," *Voprosy truda,* vyp. IV, Moscow, 1959.

26 P.S. Mstislavsky, *Narodnoye potreblenie pri sotsializme,* Moscow, 1961.

27 See I.I. Korzhenevsky, *Osnovnye zakonomernosti razvitiya sprosa v SSSR,* Moscow, 1965; P.P. Maslov, *Dokhod sovetskoi sem'i,* Moscow, 1965; I. Ya. Matyukha, *Statistika byudzhetov naseleniya,* Moscow, 1967; V.M. Sinyutin, *Na puti k ratsional'nomu potrebleniyu neprodovol'stvennykh tovarov,* Moscow, 1964; N.M. Rimashevskaya, *Ekonomicheskiy analiz dokhodov rabochikh i sluzhashchikh,* Moscow, 1965; V.V. Shvyrkov, *Zakonomernosti potrebleniya promyshlennykh i prodovol'stvennykh tovarov,* Moscow, 1965; V.F. Maier, 1. *Dokhody naseleniya i rost blagosostoyaniya naroda,* Moscow, 1968; 2. *Nekotorye metodologicheskie voprosy povysheniya zhiznennovo urovnya naroda. Izvestiya AN SSSR,* ser. ekonomika, No. 1, 1970; T.I. Nedorezova,*Metodologicheskie voprosy issledovaniya urovnya zhizni pri sotsializme. Vestnik MGU,* No. 2, 1969; *Territorial'nye problemy dokhodov i potrebleniya trudyashchikhsya,* Moscow, 1966; *Balansy dokhodov i potrebleniya naseleniya. Voprosy metodologii i statisticheskiy analiz,* Moscow, 1969, etc.

28 See, for example, O.I. Shkaratan, "Material'noye blagosostoyanie rabochevo klassa SSSR v perekohdny period ot kapitalizma k sotsializmu (po materialam Leningrada)," *Istoriya SSSR,* No. 3, 1964; N. Ya. Bromlei, "Uroven' zhizni v SSSR (1950-1965 gg.)," *Voprosy istorii,* No. 7, 1966; B.N. Kazantsev, "Rost real'noi zarabotnoi platy i dokhodov rabochikh promyshlennosti SSSR v 1951-1958 gg.," *Istoriya SSSR,* No. 3, 1966, etc.

29 *SSSR i zarubezhnye strany posle pobedy Velikoi Oktyabr'skoi sotsialisticheskoi revolyutsii. Stat. sbornik,* Moscow, 1970, p. 24.

30 See, for example, Sh. Annaklychev, *Byt i kul'tura rabochikh Turkmenistana,* Ashkhabad, 1969; A.I. Zalessky, "Ob uchenii byta rabochevo klassa v SSSR," *Voprosy istorii,* No. 5, 1955; A.S. Morozova, "Opyt izucheniya rabochevo klassa Kazakhstana," *Sovetskaya etnografiya,* No. 4, 1963; V.T. Zinich, *Sotsialisticheskie preobrazovaniya, rostki novovo, kommunisticheskovo v kul'ture i byte rabochikh sovetskoi Ukrainy,* Kiev, 1963; V.V. Mironov, *Kul'tura i byt gornyakov sovetskoi Ukrainy,* Kiev, 1965; V.M. Ivanov, *Novoye vremya – novaya zhizn' (etnografichesky ocherk o byte rabochevo klassa Belorussii perioda kommunistichekovo stroitel'stva),* Minsk, 1968; *Etnograficheskoye izuchenie sovremennovo*

byta i kul'tury rabochikh SSSR, Moscow, 1968, etc.
31 See V. Yu. Krupyanskaya, "K voprosu o problematike i metodike etnograficheskovo izucheniya sovetskovo rabochevo klassa," *Voprosy istorii,* No. 11, 1960.
32 See, for example, A.V. Orlov, *Sovremenny byt rabochei molodyozhi. Avto-ref. kand. diss.,* Kiev, 1968.
33 L.A. Anokhina, M.N. Shmeleva: 1. "Zadachi i metody etnograficheskovo izucheniya kul'tury i byta russkovo gorodskovo naseleniya (opyt izucheniya gorodov srednei polosy RSFSR)," *Sovetskaya etnografiya,* No. 6, 1966; 2. "Ispol'zovanie anketno-statisticheskikh dannykh pri etnograficheskom izuchenii goroda," *Sovetskaya etnografiya,* No. 3 1968;
   3. "K voprosu o klassifikatsii gorodskovo naseleniya pri etnograficheskom izuchenii goroda," *Sovetskaya etnografiya,* No. 2, 1970.
34 A.G. Zdravomyslov, V.P. Rozhin, V.A. Yadov (eds.), *Chelovek i yevo rabota,* Moscow, 1967.
35 See, for example, L.S. Blyakhman, A.G. Zdravomyslov, O.I. Shkalatan, *Dvizhenie rabochei sily na promyshlennykh predpriyatiyakh,* Moscow, 1965; L.S. Blyakhman, V.G. Sochilin, O.I. Shkalatan, *Podbor kadrov na predpriyatiyakh,* Moscow, 1968, etc.
36 A.G. Kharchev, *Brak i sem'ya v SSSR (opyt sotsiologicheskovo issledovaniya),* Moscow, 1964; A.G. Kharchev, K.L. Yemel'yanova, "Brak: ideal i deistvitel'nost'," *Sotsial'nye issledovaniya,* vyp. 4. *Problemy braka, sem'i i demografii,* Moscow, 1970.
37 G.A. Slesarev, *Metodologiya sotsiologicheskovo issledovaniya problem narodnonaseleniya,* Moscow, 1965.
38 *Ibid.,* p. 138.
39 On this question, see *Formy trudovoi i vnetrudovoi deyatel'nosti i sotsial'no-demograficheskie izmeneniya. Rabochiy klass i tekhnicheskiy progress. Issledovanie izmeneniy v sotsial'noi strukture rabochevo klassa,* Moscow, 1965; B.Ts. Urlanis, "Naselenie SSSR za 50 let," *Sotsial'noye issledovaniya,* vyp. 4, 1970.
40 G.A. Slesarev, Z.A. Yankova, "Zhenshchina na promyshlennom predpriyatii i v sem'ye," in G.V. Osipov and Ya. Shchepan'sky (eds.), *Sotsial'nye problemy truda i proizvodstva (sovetskopol'skoye sravnitel'noye issledovanie,* Moscow-Warsaw, 1969.
41 A.G. Kharchev, S.I. Golod: 1. "Proizvodstvennaya rabota zhenshchin i sem'ya," *Sotsial'nye problemy truda i proizvodstva,* Moscow-Warsaw, 1969; 2. *Professional'naya rabota zhenshchin i sem'ya (sotsiologicheskoye issledovanie),* Leningrad, 1971.
42 O.I. Shkaratan, *Problemy sotsial'noi struktury rabochevo klassa SSSR,* Moscow, 1970.
43 See, for example, G.S. Petrosyan, "Natsional'no-etnograficheskie razlichiya, osobennosti byta trudyashchikhsya," *Sotsial'nye issledovaniya,* vyp. 6, Moscow, 1970.
44 See G.A. Prudensky, *Vremya i trud,* Moscow, 1964; V.D. Patrushev,

Vremya kak ekonomicheskaya kategoriya, Moscow, 1966; G.N. Cherkasov, *Sotsial'no-ekonomicheskie problemy intensivnosti truda v SSSR,* Moscow, 1966; V.I. Bolgov, *Vnerabocheye vremya i uroven' zhizni trudyashchikhsya,* Novosibirsk, 1964; V.G. Kryazhev, *Vnerabocheye vremya i sfera obsluzhivaniya,* Moscow, 1966, etc.

45 *Economic Development and Cultural Change,* Chicago, Vol. 3 (October, 1954; January, 1955; April, 1955).
46 R.M. Fisher (ed.) *The Metropolis in Modern Life,* Garden City, New York, 1955.
47 *Rapport du groupe speciale d'experts de l'habitation et du developpement urban.* United Nations, New York, 1963.
48 *Urbanization in Asia and the Far East.* Proc. of the Joint UN/UNESCO Seminar, Bangkok, 8-18 August, 1956. Calcutta, 1957.
49 A. Boskoff, *The Sociology of Urban Regions,* New York, 1962, p. vii.
50 S. Greer and E. Kube, "Urbanism and Social Structure: A Los Angeles Study," in M.B. Sussman (ed.), *Community Structure and Analysis,* New York, 1959, p. 94.
51 S. Greer, *The Emerging City,* New York, 1962.
52 K. Davis, *Zarozhdenie i razvitie gorodov na zemnon share. Geografiya gorodov,* Moscow, 1965, p. 68.
53 E.W. Burgess (ed.), *Urban Community,* Chicago, 1926.
54 R.E. Park, E.W. Burgess and R.D. McKenzie, *The City,* Chicago, 1925.
55 See M. Halbwachs, *Morphologie sociale,* Paris, 1938.
56 R.S. Lynd and H.M. Lynd, *Middletown, A Study in Contemporary American Culture,* New York, 1929.
57 *Ibid.,* p. 6.
58 L. Wirth, "Urbanism as a Way of Life," *American Journal of Sociology,* Vol. 44, 1938-1939; R. Redfield, *The Folk Culture of Yucatan,* Chicago, 1941.
59 W. Firey, *Land Use in Central Boston,* Cambridge Mass., 1947; A. Hawley, *Human Ecology: a Theory of Community Structure,* New York, 1950; J.A. Quinn, *Human Ecology,* New York, 1950; R. Rossi, *Urban Residential Mobility,* New York, 1952; G.W. Breeze, *The Daytime Population in the Central Business District of Chicago,* Chicago, 1947.
60 A vast bibliography on this question is contained, for example, in the following works: H.W. Pfautz, "The Current Literature on Social Stratification: Critique and Bibliography," *American Journal of Sociology,* Vol. 58, 1952-1953, pp. 391-418; D.G. McKrae, "Bibliography on Stratification," *Current Sociology,* Vol. 2, 1953-1954, pp. 7-73.
61 See, for example, D. Riesman, *The Lonely Crowd. A Study of the Changing American Character,* New Haven, 1950; A.R. Manqus, "Personality Adjustment of Rural and Urban Children," *American Sociological Review,* Vol. 13, 1948; A. Kornhauser, *Detroit as People See It: a Survey of Attitudes in an Industrial City,* Detroit, 1952.
62 D.L. Foley, *Neighbours or Urbanites?* Rochester, New York, 1952; R. Deutschberger, "Interaction Patterns in Changing Neighbourhoods,"

Sociometry Monographs, No. 18, Beacon, New York, 1947.

63 L. Wirth, "Housing as a Field of Sociological Research," *American Sociological Review,* Vol. 12, 1947; C. Abrams, *Forbidden Neighbours,* New York, 1955; E. Higbee, *The Squeeze. Cities without Space,* New York, 1960.

64 R.C. Angell, "The Moral Integration of American Cities," Special Supplement. *American Journal of Sociology,* Vol. 57, 1951-1952.

65 C.W. Mills et al., *The Puerto Rican Journey,* New York, 1950; A. Gordon, *Jews in Transition,* Minneapolis, 1949; St. C. Drake and H.R. Clayton, *Black Metropolis,* New York, 1945.

66 N.P. Gist, "The Urban Community," in J.B. Gittler (ed.), *Review of Sociology. Analysis of a Decade,* New York, 1957, p. 177.

67 G.Sjoberg: 1. "Theory and Research in Urban Sociology," in P.M. Hauser and L.F. Shnore (ed.), *The Study of Urbanization,* New York, 1967; 2. "The Rise and Fall of Cities: a Theoretical Perspective," *International Journal of Comparative Sociology,* Vol. 4, 1963; 3. "Cities in Developing and Industrial Societies: a Cross-Cultural Analysis," in *The Study of Urbanization.*

68 G. Sjoberg, "Theory and Research in Urban Sociology," p. 159.

69 N. Babchuk and C.W. Gordon, "The Voluntary Association in the Slum," *University of Nebraska Studies,* No. 27, 1962; H.J. Gans, *The Urban Villagers,* New York, 1962.

70 O. Lewis, "Urbanization without Breakdown: a Case Study," *Scientific Monthly,* No. 75, 1952.

71 A.L. Epstein, *Politics in an Urban African Community,* Manchester, 1958; P. Marris, *Family and Social Change in an African City,* Evanston, 1962.

72 J. Bensman and B. Rosenberg, *Mass, Class and Bureaucracy,* Englewood Cliffs, New York, 1963.

73 O.D. Duncan and A.J. Reiss, *Social Characteristics of Urban and Rural Communities,* New York, 1956.

74 O.D. Duncan and L.F. Schnore, "Cultural Behaviour and Ecological Perspectives in the Study of Social Organization," *American Journal of Sociology,* Vol. 65, 1959.

75 J.P. Gibbs and W.T. Martin, "Urbanization, Technology and the Division of Labour. International Patterns," *American Sociological Review,* Vol. 27, 1962.

76 G. Sjoberg, "Theory and Research in Urban Sociology," *op. cit.,* pp. 168-169.

77 E. Shevsky and W. Bell, *Social Area Analysis: Theory, Illustrative Application and Computational Procedures,* Standford, 1955.

78 S. Greer, *The Emerging City, op. cit.*

79 L. Mumford: 1. "The Automation of Knowledge (Are we becoming robots?)," *Vital Speeches of the Day,* Vo. 30, No. 4, 1964; 2. *The City in History. Its Origins, its Transformations and its Prospects,* New York, 1961; 3. *Technics and Civilisation,* New York, 1934; 4. *The Culture of Cities,* New York, 1938; 5. *In the Name of Sanity,* New York, 1954.

80 G. Sjoberg, "Sravnitel'naya urbanistskaya sotsiologiya," *Sotsiologiya sevodnya,* Moscow, 1965.
81 G. Sjoberg, "Theory and Research in Urban Sociology," *op. cit.*
82 W.F. Ogburn, "Inventions of Local Transportation and Patterns of Cities," in P.K. Hatt and A.J. Reiss (eds.), *Cities and Society: the Revised Reader in Urban Sociology,* New York, 1957.
83 This question is dealt with more fully in G. Sjoberg, "Sravnitel'naya urbanistskaya sotsiologiya," *op. cit.,* pp. 384-390.
84 M. Weber, *The City,* New York, 1958.
85 R.E. Dickinson, *The West European City,* London, 1951.
86 W.L. Kolb, "The Social Structure and Function of Cities," *Economic Development and Cultural Change,* Vol. 3, 1954.
87 W. Form, "The Place of Social Structure in the Determination of Land Use: Some Implications for Theory of Urban Ecology," *Social Forces,* Vol. 32, 1954.
88 P.H. Chaumbart de Lauwe et al., *Paris et l'agglomeration parisienne,* Paris, 1952.
89 P. George, *Etudes sur la banlieue de Paris,* Paris, 1950.
90 *Daseinformen der Grossstadt. Typische Formen sozialer Existens in Stadtmitte. Vorstadt und Gurtel der industriellen Grossstadt,* Tubingen, 1959.
91 H.P. Bahrdt, *Die moderne Grossstadt. Soziologische Uberlegungen zum Stadtebau,* Rowohlt, 1961.
92 A.C. Hofmann, D. Kersten, *Frauen zwischen Familie und Fabrik. Die Doppelbelastung der Frau durch Haushalt und Beruf,* Munich, 1958.
93 N. Anderson, *The Urban Community; a World Perspective,* London, 1960; J.N. Nicholson, *New Communities in Britain. Achievements and Problems,* London, 1961.
94 See W.J.H. Sprott, "Sotsiologiya v Anglii: osnovnaya tematika," in H. Becker and A. Boskoff, *Sovremennaya sotsiologicheskaya teoriya v yeyo preyemstvennost' i izmenenii,* Moscow, 1961, pp. 693-697. See also such works as H. Bracey, *Neighbours: Neighbouring and Neighbourliness on New Estates and Subdivisions in England and the U.S.A.,* London, 1964; W. Ashworth, *The Genesis of Modern British Town Planning: a Study in Economic and Social History of the Nineteenth and Twentieth Centuries,* London, 1965.
95 F. Zweig, *The Worker in an Affluent Society. Family Life and Industry,* London, 1961.
96 M. Young and P. Willmott, *Family and Kinship in East London,* London, 1957.
97 See K. Odaka, "Sotsiologiya v Yaponii: akkomodatsiya zapadnykh vozzrenny," in Becker and Boskoff, *op. cit.,* pp. 824-825; T. Yazaki, *Social Change and the City in Japan: from Earliest Times through the Industrial Revolution,* Tokyo, 1968.
98 R.P. Dore, *City Life in Japan: a Study of a Tokyo Ward,* London (2nd impression), 1963.

99 See M.R. Stein, *The Eclipse of Community*, Princeton, 1960.
100 V.I. Lenin, *Collected Works* (Russian), Vol. 30, p. 350.

Chapter 3   **Soviet Urban Research**

1   For more details on the programme and methods of this investigation, see O.I. Shkaratan, *Problemy sotsial'noi struktury rabochevo klassa (istoriko-sotsiologicheskoye issledovanie)*, Moscow, 1970, pp. 178-187.
2   For more detail, see O.I. Shkaratan, *op. cit.*, pp. 188-190.
3   For sample estimate and measurement of its accuracy, see E.K. Vasilieva, "Etno-demograficheskaya kharakteristika semeinoi struktury naseleniya Kazani v 1967 g.," *Sovetskaya etnografiya*, No. 5, 1968, pp. 13-14.
4   *Pravda*, 27 September, 1967.
5   *Loc. cit.*
6   *Pravda*, 30 December, 1968.
7   See *Materialy XXIV s'yezda KPSS*, Moscow, 1971, p. 40.
8   *Ibid.*, pp. 176-178.
9   "Ob itogakh vypolneniya Gosudarstvennovo plana razvitiya narodnovo khozyaistva SSSR v 1970 godu. Soobshchenie TsSU SSSR," *Pravda*, 4 February, 1971.
10 *Loc. cit.*
11 P.P. Maslov, *Dopolnitel'nye dokhody rabochikh. Metodologicheskie voprosy izucheniya urovnya trudyashchikhsya*, Moscow, 1959, p. 123.
12 A.S. Koval'chuk, "Sushchnost' obshchestvennykh fondov lichnovo potrebleniya pri sotsializme," *Voprosy filosofii*, No. 3, 1969, p. 31.
13 "Ob itogakh vypolneniya Gosudarstvennovo plana razvitiya narodnovo khozyaistva SSSR v 1970 godu . . . " *op. cit.*
14 *Narodnoye khozyaistvo SSSR v 1969 g. Stat. yezhegodnik*, Moscow, 1970, p. 538.
15 *Ibid.*
16 Calculation was made from the statistical yearly *Narodnoye khozyaistvo SSSR v 1969 g.*, p. 560.
17 See *Materialy XXIV s'yezda KPSS*, p. 178.
18 *Narodnoye khozyaistvo SSSR v 1969 g.*, p. 598.
19 Calculation was made from *Narodnoye khozyaistvo SSSR v 1969 g.*, p. 626.
20 See *Pravda*, 1 March, 1971.
21 See *My i planeta (tsifry i fakty)*, Moscow, 1969, pp. 173-176.
22 *Ibid.*, p. 169.
23 *SSSR i zarubezhnye strany posle pobedy Velikoi Oktyabr'skoi sotsialisicheskoi revolyutsii. Stat. sbornik*, Moscow, 1970, p. 177.
24 See *My i planeta*, pp. 170-173.
25 See *Narodnoye khozyaistvo SSSR v 1969 g.*, p. 598.
26 *Pravda*, 10 March, 1967.
27 *Pravda*, 14 February, 1971.
28 *Pravda*, 5 June, 1970.

29   Of course, data on extent of isolation do not give an exhaustive description of housing conditions. The quality of living space also depends on how well it is equipped, the materials from which it is made, etc. We shall not, however, be looking at this question here.
30   V.I. Lenin *Collected Works*(Russian), Vol. 6, p. 232.
31   For more detail, see *Kommunism i kul'tura. Zakonomernosti formirovaniya i razvitiya novoi kul'tury*, Moscow, 1966; *Stroitel'stvo kommunizma i dukhovniy mir cheloveka*, Moscow, 1966, etc.
32   *Trud v SSSR. Spravochnik. 1926-1930 gg.*, Moscow, 1930, pp. XVI-XVII.
33   "Gordoye zvanie – rabochiy. Zametki s plenuma Leningradskovo obkoma KPSS," *Leningradskaya pravda*, 7 February, 1969.
34   *Leningrad za 50 let. Stat. sbornik*, Leningrad, 1967, p. 85.
35   *Ibid.*
36   "Ob itigakh vypolneniya gosudarstvennovo plana razvitiya narodnovo khozyaistva Leningrada i Leningradshoi oblasti za 1968 i 1969 gg. Soobshchenie statisticheskikh upravleniy goroda Leningrada i Leningradskoi oblasti 1968 g.," *Leningradskaya pravda*, 14 January, 1969 and 16 January, 1970.
37   *Loc. cit.*
38   *Loc. cit.*
39   *Loc. cit.*
40   *My i planeta*, p. 169.
41   "Ob itigakh vypolneniya . . . " *Leningradskaya pravda, op. cit.*
42   *Loc. cit.*
43   V.A. Yezhov, "O roli rabochevo klassa v kul'turnom razvitii sovetskovo obshchestva," in *Rabochiy klass SSSR na sovremennom etape*, Leningrad, 1968, p. 56.
44   The table was compiled by I.V. Ryabikova and V.A. Petrov, to whom we acknowledge our debt.
45   See *Helping the Family in Urban Society*, New York – London, 1963, p. 7; S.K. Weinberg, *Social Problems in Our Time. A Sociological Analysis.* Englewood Cliffs, New York, 1960, p. 19.
46   The sample included persons solely concerned with the home. In that connection, we may note that the average size of family and number of members with independent earnings fully coincide in 1965 and 1970.
47   A.G. Kharchev, *Brak i sem'ya v SSSR*, Moscow, 1964, p. 224.
48   V.I. Lenin *Collected Works* (Russian), Vol. 37, p. 185.
49   *Ibid.*
50   L.S. Blyakhman, A.G. Zdravomyslov, O.I. Shkaratan, *Dvizhenie rabochei sily na promyshlennykh predpriyatiyakh*, Moscow, 1965, p. 65.
51   *Ibid.*, p. 66.
52   Thus, for example, F. Zweig has noted that the overwhelming majority of women in British industry are semi-skilled workers (F. Zweig, *The Worker in an Affluent Society*, London, 1961, p. 171). Talking of the status of

American working women, B. Gardner says that entrepreneurs regard them as low-grade manpower deprived of promotion opportunities (B.B. Gardner, *Human Relations in Industry,* Chicago, 1946, p. 267). He stresses that the normal role-expectation of women in American society is to be a wife or mother, which is the basic centre of their interests (*ibid.,* p. 172).

53   On this question, see Z.A. Yankova, "O semeino-bytovykh rolyakh rabotayushchei zhenshchiny," *Sotsial'nye issledovaniya,* vyp, 4, *Problemy braka, sem'yi i demografii,* Moscow, 1970; A.G. Kharchev, S.I. Golod, *Professional'naya rabota zhenshchin i sem'ya (sotsiologicheskoye issledovanie),* Leningrad, 1971.
54   A.G. Zdravomyslov, V.A. Yadov, "Otnoshenie k trudu i tsennostnye orientatsii lichnosti," in *Sotsiologiya v SSSR,* Vol. 2, Moscow, 1966, pp. 202-203.
55   N.K. Krupskaya, *O kommunisticheskom vospitanii,* Moscow, 1956, p. 340.
56   See *Narodnoye khozyaistvo SSSR v 1969 g.,* pp. 659-661.
57   *Pravda,* 14 February, 1971.

Chapter 4   Cumulative Methods of Investigating Everyday Life

1   The registration card was developed in the sociological research laboratory of Leningrad State University. See *Metodika izucheniya byudzhetov vremeni trudyashchikhsya (sbornik materialov),* Novosibirsk, 1966, pp. 181-186.
2   We acknowledge our gratitude to B.L. Spektor, chief of the Scientific Organisation of Labour bureau, and to his co-workers N.I. Makarova and T.T. Kapitonova, who did much of the work in collecting and preparing the primary material for machine processing.
3   V.I. Lenin, *Collected Works* (Russian), Vol. 36, p. 192.
4   E. Belyayev, V. Vodzinskaya et al., "Izuchenie byudzheta vremeni trudyashchikhsya kak odin iz metodov konkretno-sotsiologicheskovo issledovaniya," *Vestnik LGU,* No. 23, 1961, p. 100
5   On this question, see, for example, L. Sinetar, "Svobodnoye vremya i vliyanie bytovykh tovarov na yevo uvelichenie," *Ekonomika Sovetskoi Ukrainy,* No. 1, 1970.
6   Belyayev, Vodzinskaya, *op. cit.,* p. 102.
7   The bourgeois sociologist S. de Grazia notes that an opinion exists today in the West that time spent on watching TV is a passive form of leisure. See S. de Grazia, *Of Time, Work and Leisure,* New York, 1962, p. 333.
8   In this connection, let us note that according to research carried out in several American cities (Chicago, San Francisco, Dallas and Atlanta), one fifth of the 192 hours of TV programmes provided a motive for crime. See M. Kaplan, *Leisure in America. A Social Inquiry,* New York, 1960, p. 224.
9   M. Santo, "Nekotorye predvaritel'nye itogi izucheniya svobodnovo vremeni," *Problemy mira i sotsializma.* Supplement to No. 6, 1965, p. 14.
10   For more detail, see B.G. Ananiev, "Chelovek kak predmet vospitaniya

	(perspektivy pedagogicheskoi antropologii)," *Sovetskaya pedagogika*, No. 1, 1965.
11	N. Anderson, *Work and Leisure*, London, 1961, p. 83.
12	G.V. Osipov, S.F. Frolov, "Vnerabocheye vremya i yevo ispol'zovanie," in *Sotsiologiya v SSSR*, Vol. 2, Moscow, 1966, pp. 235-236.
13	See V.D. Patrushev, "Byudzhet vremeni gorodskovo naseleniya sotsialisticheskikh i kapitalisticheskikh stran," *Filosofskie nauki*, No. 5, 1968, p. 56.
14	Such surveys have not gained much popularity abroad either. Only a few works concerned with sociological analysis of the home conditions of the modern worker pay attention to particular items of household use. Most often, research is focused on the television or the car and their significance in changing the lives and leisure of modern workers. See, for example, M. Kaplan, *Leisure in America*, New York, 1960; F. Zweig, *The Worker in an Affluent Society*, London, 1961.
15	See *Instruktsiya po obsledovaniyu byudzhetov rabochikh i sluzhashchikh*, Moscow, Izd. TsSU SSSR, 1968.
16	According to information from other works, there is also quite a strong desire to acquire one's 'own transport', particularly a car. See, for example, V.B. Ol'shansky, "Lichnost' i sotsial'nye tsennosti," in *Sotsiologiya v SSSR*, Vol. 1, Moscow, 1966, p. 487.
17	See *Materialy XXIV s'yezda KPSS*, Moscow, 1971, p. 151.
18	S.G. Strumilin, *Problemy ekonomiki truda*, Moscow, 1964, p. 259.
19	*Ibid.*
20	Z.A. Yankova, "O semeino-bytovykh rolyakh rabotayushchei zhenshchiny," *Sotsial'nye issledovaniya*, vyp. 4, Moscow, 1970, p. 78; A.G. Kharchev, S.I. Golod: 1. "Proizvodstvennaya rabota zhenshchin i sem'ya," in *Sotsial'nye problemy truda i proizvodstva*, Moscow-Warsaw, 1969; 2. *Professional'naya rabota zhenshchin i sem'ya (sotsiologicheskoye issledovanie)*, Leningrad, 1971.
21	G.S. Petrosyan, *Vnerabocheye vremya trudyashchikhsya v SSSR*, Moscow, 1965, p. 120.
22	See Yu. A. Zamochkin, L.N. Zhilina, N.T. Frolova, "Sdvigi v massovom potreblenii i lichnost'," *Voprosy filosofii*, 1969, No. 6, p. 30.

Conclusions

1 *Pravda*, 14 February, 1971.
2 V.I. Lenin, *Collected Works* (Russian), Vol. 44, p. 170.
3 *Pravda*, 21 March, 1972.
4 *Materialy XXIV s'yezda KPSS*, Moscow, 1971, p. 72.

SPECIAL SECTION

Bibliography

Soviet literature on urbanisation published since 1960. Many other references to pre- and post-revolutionary works are included in the Notes. (This is a special section compiled by the translator and not part of Trufanov's book.)

Section 1.   On the USSR

Akhiezer, A.S., "Nauchno-tekhnicheskaya revolyutsia i upravlenie razvitiem obshchestva," *Voprosy filosofii,* No. 8, 1968.
Akhiezer, A.S., "Nekotorye voprosy metodologii gradostroitel'noi nauki," *Arkhitektura SSSR,* No. 2, 1968.
Akhiezer, A.S., "Nekotorye problemy sotsial'nykh issledovaniy goroda," in *Nauchnye prognozy razvitiya i formirovaniya sovetskikh gorodov na baze sotsial'novo i nauchno-tekhnicheskovo progressa,* vyp. 2, Moscow, 1969.
Akhiezer, A.S., "Rabochiy klass i upravlenie urbanizatsiei," in *Urbanizatsiya i rabochiy klass v ulooviakh nauchno-tekhnicheskoi revolyutsii,* Sovetskiy fond mira, Moscow, 1970.
Akhiezer, A.S., Kogan, L.B., Yanitsky, O.N. "Urbanisatsiya, obshchestvo i nauchno-tekhnickeskaya revolyutsiya," *Voprosy filosofii,* No. 2, 1969.
Akhiezer, A.S., Kochetov, A.V. *Nekotorye zakonomernosti urbanizatsii i yeyo prognoz v SSSR,* Moscow, 1970.
Akhiezer, A.S., Kochetov, A.V., Yargina, Z.N., "Problemy prognozirovaniya gorodskikh poseleniy," in *Materialy po naukovedeniyu.* III Kievsky simpozium po naukovedeniyu i nauchno-tekhnicheskomu prognozirovaniyu. Tezisy dokladov. Vyp.   7, Kiev, 1970.
Akhmedov, E.A., Fatakhov, Ye. N., *Novye goroda Uzbekistana,* Tashkent, 1972.
Badamyan, I.A., "Sotsial'noye soderzhanie problemy kachestva massovovo gorodskovo zhilishcha," in *Arkhitekturno-sotsiologicheskie issledovaniya (Obzor),* vyp. 1, Moscow, 1970.
Badamyan, I.A., "Urbanizatsiya i problema vospriozvodstva naseleniya," in *Urbanizatsiya i rabochiy klass v usloviakh nauchno-tekhnicheskoi revolyutsii,* Moscow, 1970.
Baranov, A.V., "Molodyozh' i urbanizatsiya," in *Chelovek i obshchestvo. Sotsial'nye problemy molodyozhi.* Leningrad Univ., 1969.
Baranov, A.V., *O sotsial'noi modeli zhilishcha sotsialisticheskovo urbanizirovannovo obshchestva,* Moscow, 1970.
Baranov, A.V., "Urbanizatsiya i zhilishche," in *Urbanizatsiya i rabochiy klass v usloviakh nauchno-tekhnicheskoi revolyutsii,* Moscow, 1970.
Blinkova, L.M., "K voprosu a razvitii gorodov Podmoskov'ya, *Problemy sovetskovo gradostroitel'stva,* No. 13, 1961.
Bocharov, Yu. P., Rabinovich, V.I., "Stroitel'stvo kommunizma i problemy razvitiya nashikh gorodov," *Voprosy filosofii,* No. 2, 1962.
Bogorad, D.I., "Zadachi izucheniya i regulirovaniya rosta gorodskikh aglomeratsiy," *Nauchnye problemy geografii naseleniya,* Moscow Univ., 1967.

Bolgov, V.I. (ed.), *Sotsial'nye issledovaniya. Problemy byudzheta vremeni trudyashchikhsya,* vyp. 6, Moscow, 1970.
Bonifatyeva, L.I., Pokshishevsky, V.V., "Urbanizatsiya," *Kratkaya geograficheskaya entsiklopediya,* Vol. 5, Moscow, 1966, pp. 189-190.
Borisevich, Ye. A., "O nekotorykh sotsiologicheskikh predposylkakh formirovaniya struktury sotsialisticheskovo goroda," in *Arkhitektura. Materialy k XXIX nauchnoi konferentsii LISI* (1-6 February, 1971), Leningrad, 1971.
Davidovich, V.G., "Velichina gorodskikh poseleniy SSSR," *Voprosy geografii,* No. 56, Moscow, 1962.
Davidovich, V.G., "Gorodskie aglomeratsii v SSSR," *Voprosy gorodskovo rasseleniya,* Kiev, 1964.
Davidovich, V.G., "Vystuplenie na zasedanii seminara po urbanizatsii," *Geografiya naseleniya,* vyp. 4, Moscow, 1970.
Davidovich, V.G., "O kolichestvennykh zakonomerostyakh urbanizatsii v SSSR," in *Problemy urbanizatsii v SSSR.* Moscow Univ., 1971.
Dolgy, V.M., Levinson, A.G., "Arkhaicheskaya kul'tura i gorod," *Voprosy filosofii,* No. 7, 1971.
Gokhman, V.M. "Urbanizatsiya i rost gorodov," in *Urbanizatsiya i rabochiy klass v usloviakh nauchno-tekhnicheskoi revolyutsii,* Moscow, 1970.
Gokhman, V.M., Karpov, L.N., "Goroda i razmeshchenie proizvodstva," *Mirovaya ekonomika i mezhdunarodnye otnosheniya,* No. 3, 1970.
Gordon, L.A., Klopov, E.V., *Chelovek posle raboty. Sotsial'nye problemy byta i vnerabochevo vremeni,* Moscow, 1972.
Gordon, L.A., Rimashevskaya, N.M., *Pyatidnevnaya rabochaya nedelya i svobodnoye vremya trudyashchikhsya,* Moscow, 1972.
Ioppe, V.I., *Urbanizatsiya Severa,* Moscow, 1969.
Ivanov, V., "Urbanizatsiya: nastoyashcheye i budushcheye. Konferentsiya v IMRD," *Voprosy ekonomiki,* No. 11, 1969.
Kagan, M.I., "O dinamike podvizhnosti gorodskovo naseleniya," in *Razvitie sistemy gorodskovo transporta,* vyp. 4, Kiev, 1971.
Kagan, M.I., "Urbanizatsiya, prostranstvennaya mobil'nost', podvizhnost'," in *Urbanizatsiya i rabochiy klass v usloviakh nauchno-tekhnicheskoi revolyutsii,* Moscow, 1970.
Kaplan, G.A., "Ekonomicheskie prognozy perspektivnovo rasseleniya," in *Nauchnye prognozy razvitiya i formirovaniya sovetskikh gorodov na baze sotsial'novo i nauchno-tekhnicheskovo progressa,* vyp. 3, Moscow, 1969.
Khodzhayev, D.G., Khorev, B.S., "Kontesptsii yedinoi sistemy rasseleniya i planovoye regulirovanie rosta gorodov v SSSR," in *Problemy urbanizatsii v SSSR,* Moscow Univ., 1971.
Khorev, B.S., *Gorodskoye poseleniya SSSR,* Moscow, 1968.
Khorev, B.S., "Rasselenie i territorial'no-sistemnaya organizatsiya proizvoditel'nykh sil (voprosy teorii rasseleniya)," *Izvestiya AN SSSR. Seriya geograficheskaya,* No. 2, 1971.
Kogan, L.B., "O sotsial'no-informatsionnom aspekte urbanizatsii," *Sotsial'nye problemy zhilishcha. Sbornik nauchnykh soobshcheniy,* Leningrad, 1969.

Kogan, L.B., "O roli sotsiologicheskikh faktorov v formirovanii material'noprostranstvennoi sredy goroda," in *Nauchnye prognozy razvitiya i formirovaniya sovetskikh gorodov na baze sotsial'novo i nauchnotekhnicheskovo progressa,* vyp. 2, Moscow, 1969.
Kogan, L.B., "Sootnoshenie planirovochnykh yedinits i struktury goroda," *Arkhitektura SSSR,* No. 6, 1970.
Kogan, L.B., "Urbanizatsiya," *Filosofskaya entsiklopediya,* Vol. 5, Moscow, 1970.
Kogan, L.B., *Urbanizatsiya i gorodskaya kul'tura,* Moscow, 1970.
Kogan, L.B., "Urbanizatsiya i kul'tura goroda (tendentsiya i mekhanizmy)," in *Urbanizatsiya i rabochiy klass v usloviakh nauchno-tekhnicheskoi revolyutsii,* Moscow, 1970.
Kogan, L.B., "Urbanizatsiya – obshchenie – mikroraion," *Arkhitektura SSSR,* No. 4, 1967.
Kogan, L.B., Kolbanovsky, V.V., Yanitsky, O.N., "Sotsial'nye problemy urbanizatsii," in *Sotsiologicheskie issledovaniya goroda,* Moscow, 1969.
Kogan, L.B., Loktev, V.I., "Nekotorye sotsiologicheskie aspekty modelirovaniya gorodov," *Voprosy filosofii,* No. 9, 1964.
Kolpakov, B.T., Patrushev, V.D. (eds.), *Byudzhet vremeni gorodskovo naseleniya,* Moscow, 1971.
Kozlov, V.I., "Etnogeograficheskie aspekty urbanizatsii v SSSR," in *Geograficheskie aspekty urbanizatsii,* Moscow, 1971.
Kudryavtsev, O.K., "Urbanizatsiya v sovremennom mire," *Chetvorty seminar po voprosam gorodskovo dvizheniya. Materialy k dokladam,* Moscow, 1968.
Kurman, M.V., "Urbanizatsiya i problema sootvetstviya vozrastno-polovykh struktur zanyatykh i nalichnykh trudovykh resursov," in *Materialy Vsesoyuznoi nauchnoi konferentsii po problemam narodno-naseleniya Zakavkaz'ya.* Yerevan, 1968.
Kurman, M.V., Lebedinsky, I.V., *Naselenie bol'shovo sotsialisticheskovo goroda,* Moscow, 1968.
Lappo, G.M., "O problemakh rasseleniya Bol'shoi Moskvy," *Gorodskoye khozyaistvo Moskvy,* No. 7, 1961.
Lappo, G.M., "Izuchenie gorodskikh aglomeratsiy," *Sovetskaya geografiya v period stroitel'stva kommunizma,* Moscow, 1963.
Lappo, G.M., Pivovarov, Yu. L., "Urbanizatsiya i prirodnaya sreda," in *Geograficheskie aspekty urbanizatsii,* Moscow, 1971.
Larmin, O.V., Moiseyenko, V.M., Khorev, B.S., "Sotsial'no-demograficheskie aspekty urbanizatsii v SSSR," in *Problemy urbanizatsii v SSSR,* Moscow Univ., 1971.
Lavrov, V.A., "Goroda manyayut svoyu strukturu," *Arkhitektura SSSR,* No. 11, 1966.
Lavrov, V.A., "Puti preobrazovaniya planirovochnoi struktury gorodov," in *Nauchnye prognozy razvitiya i formirovaniya sovetskikh gorodov na baze sotsial'novo i nauchno-tekhnicheskovo progressa,* vyp. 1, Moscow, 1968.
Mayergoiz, I.M., et al., "Geograficheskie aspekty urbanizatsii," in *Problemy urbanizatsii v SSSR,* Moscow Univ., 1971.

Mishchenko, G. Ye., "Regulirovanie rosta naseleniya Moskvy i yevo rasselenie," *Gorodskoye khozyaistvo Moskvy,* No. 3, 1961.
Moskvin, D.D., "Razmeshchenie naseleniya i trudovykh resursov, ikh rol' v spetsializatsii i kompleksnom razvitii khozyaistva ekonomicheskikh raionov," in *Zakonomernosti i faktory razvitiya ekonomicheskikh raionov SSSR,* Moscow, 1965.
Novy element rasseleniya, Gosstroiizdat, Moscow, 1966.
Nymmik, S. Ya., "O yadrakh raionoobrazovaniya," *Vestnik MGU.* Seriya V. Geografiya, No. 1, 1970.
Osidze, A.F., "Mesto nebol'shikh gorodskikh poseleniy v urbanizatsii SSSR," in *Problemy razvitiya gorodov i ispol'zovanie trudovykh resursov,* Moscow, 1968.
Osipov, G.V., "Sotsiologicheskie aspekty urbanizatsii," in *Problemy sovetskovo gradostroitel'stva,* vyp. 2, Kiev, 1971.
Palvanova, Z., "Gorod i kul'tura," *Dekorativnoye iskussva SSSR,* No. 2, 1970.
Palynsh, R., "V.I. Lenin o roli gorodov v razvitii obshchestva i problema sushchnosti urbanizatsii," *Voprosy filosofskovo naslediya V.I. Lenina,* Riga, 1970.
Pchelintsev, O.S., "Znachenie goroda (urbanizirovannovo raiona) v sisteme razmeshcheniya proizvodstva," in *Urbanizatsiya i rabochiy klass v usloviakh nauchno-tekhnicheskoi revolyutsii,* Moscow, 1970.
Pchelintsev, O.S., "Problemy razvitiya bol'shikh gorodov," in *Sotsiologiya v SSSR,* Vol. 2, Moscow, 1966.
Pivovarov, Yu. L., "Urbanizatsiya i nauchno-tekhnicheskaya revolyutsia," *Izvestiya AN SSSR.* Seriya geograficheskaya, No. 2, 1970.
Pivovarov, Yu. L., "Urbanizatsiya i territorial'naya struktura khozyaistva," in *Urbanizatsiya i rabochiy klass v usloviakh nauchno-tekhnicheskoi revolyutsii,* Moscow, 1970.
Pivovarov, Yu. L., (ed.), *Problemy sovremennoi urbanizatsii,* Moscow, 1972.
Pokshishevsky, V.V., "Vystuplenie na zasedanii seminara po urbanizatsii," in *Geografiya naseleniya,* vyp. 4, Moscow, 1970.
Pokshishevsky, V.V., "Etnicheskie protsessy v gorodakh SSSR i nekotorye problemy ikh izucheniya," *Sovetskaya etnografiya,* No. 5, 1969.
Pokshishevsky, V.V., "Urbanizatsiya i etnogeograficheskie protsessy," in *Problemy urbanizatsii v SSSR,* Moscow Univ., 1971.
Prudensky, G.A. *Vremya i trud,* Moscow, 1965.
Puti razvitiya malykh i srednykh gorodov tsentral'nykh ekonomicheskikh raionov SSSR, Moscow, 1967.
Rodoman, B.B., "Nekotorye puti sokhraneniya biosfery pri urbanizatsii," *Vestnik MGU.* Seriya V. Geografiya, No. 3, 1971.
Rumyantsev, A.M., "Urbanizatsiya i obshchestvo," in *Urbanizatsiya i rabochiy klass v usloviakh nauchno-tekhnicheskoi revolyutsii,* Moscow, 1970.
Ruzavina, Ye. I., "Ekonomicheskie storony protsessa urbanizatsii," *Nauchnye doklady vysshei shkoly.* Ekonomicheskie nauki, No. 2, 1969.
Ryabushkin, T.V. (ed.), *Izuchenie vosproizvodstva naseleniya,* Moscow.

Saifullina, F.A., "Protsess urbanizatsii i trudovye resursy," *Trudy Kazanskovo aviatsionnovo instituta,* vyp. 100, 1970.
Shakhot'ko, L.P., "Vliyanie urbanizatsii na uroven' rozhdayemosti v Belorusskoi SSSR," in *Problemy narodonaseleniya i trudovykh resursov,* vyp. 2, Minsk, 1971.
Sokolov, N.B., "Nekotorye voprosy izucheniya urbanizatsii kak sotsial'novo protsessa," in *Urbanizatsiya i rabochiy klass v usloviakh nauchno-tekhnicheskoi revolyutsii,* Moscow, 1970.
Soldatov, S.I., "Formirovanie perspektivnykh sistem rasseleniya," in *Nauchnye prognozy razvitiya i formirovaniya sovetskikh gorodov na baze sotial'novo i nauchno-tekhnicheskovo progressa,* vyp. 3, Moscow, 1969.
Solofnenko, N.A., "Nekotorye voprosy urbanizatsii i razvitiya rasseleniya," in *Gradostroitel'stvo i raionnaya planirovka,* vyp. 7, Kiev, 1967.
Solofnenko, N.A., "Prognoz razvitiya perspektivnykh form i sistem rasseleniya," in *Nauchnye prognozy razvitiya i formirovaniya sovetskikh gorodov na baze sotial'novo i nauchno-tekhnicheskovo progressa,* vyp. 3, Moscow, 1969.
Solovyov, N. et al., *Problemy byta, braka i sem'yi,* Vilnius, 1970.
"Sotsial'nye predposylki formirovaniya goroda budushchevo," *Tsentr nauchno tekhnicheskoi informatsii po grazhdanskomu stroitel'stvu i arkhitekture,* vyp. 31, Moscow, 1967.
Staroverov, V.I., *Gorod ili derevnya,* Moscow, 1972.
Stolyar, I.M., "Sotsial'nye predposylki formirovaniya struktury goroda v epokhu nauchno-tekhnicheskoi revolyutsii," in *Nauchnye prognozy razvitiya i formirovaniya sovetskikh gorodov na baze sotsial'novo i nauchno-tekhnicheskovo progressa,* vyp. 1, Moscow, 1968.
Stolyar, I.M., *Sotsial'no-prostranstvennaya model' goroda,* Moscow, 1970.
Strongina, M.L., "Problemy razvitiya bol'shikh gorodov i aglomeratsiy," *Sotsial'nye issledovaniya,* vyp. 4, Moscow, 1970.
Strongina, M.L., *Sotsial'no-ekonomicheskie problemy razvitiya bol'shikh gorodov v SSSR,* Moscow, 1970.
Taborisskaya, I.M., "Protsess kosvennoi urbanizatsii i yevo znachenie," in *Gradostroitel'stvo. Problemy razvitiya gorodov,* Kiev, 1970.
Tatevosov, R.B., "Metody analiza mezhraionnoi migratsii v SSSR v svyazi s protsessom urbanizatsii," in *Problemy urbanizatsii v SSSR,* Moscow Univ., 1971.
Valentei, D.I., (ed.), *Marksistsko-leninskaya teoriya narodnaseleniya,* Moscow, 1971 (see Chapter on Problemy sovremennoi urbanizatsii).
Valentei, D.L., *Teoriya i politika narodnoaseleniya,* Moscow, 1967.
Vasilieva, E.K., *Sotsial'no-professional'ny uroven' gorodskoi molodyozhi,* Leningrad Univ., 1973.
Vinogradov, N.A., Deryabina, V.L., *Urbanizatsiya i zdorov'ye,* Moscow, 1970.
Yanitsky, O.N., "Gorod kak informatsionnaya sistema," in *Sotsiologicheskie issledovaniya goroda,* Moscow, 1969.
Yanitsky, O.N., "K probleme upravleniya gorodom kak sistemoi," in *Kolichestvannye metody v sotsial'nykh issledovaniyakh,* Moscow, 1968.

Yanitsky, O.N., "Simpozium po problemam urbanizatsii," *Voprosy filosofii,* No. 10, 1969.
Yanitsky, O.N., "Sovetsky gorod kak ob'yekt sotsiologicheskovo issledovaniya," in *Arkhitekturno-sotsiologicheskie issledovaniya. (Obzor),* vyp. 1, Moscow, 1970.
Yanitsky, O.N., "Sotsial'nye problemy urbanizatsii," in *Teoreticheskie problemy sovetskoi arkhitektury. Materialy k seminaru,* Moscow, 1969.
Yanitsky, O.N., *Sotsial'no-informatsionnye aspekty urbanizatsii,* Moscow, 1970.
Yanitsky, O.N., "Sotsiologicheskie issledovaniya i prostranstvennoye proyektirovanie," in *Nauchnye prognozy razvitiya i formirovaniya sovetskikh gorodov na baze sotsial'novo i nauchno-tekhnicheskovo progressa,* vyp. 2, Moscow, 1969.
Yanitsky, O.N., "Tendentsii urbanizatsii v usloviakh nauchno-tekhnicheskoi revolyutsii," in *Geograficheskie aspekty urbanizatsii,* Moscow, 1971.
Yargina, Z.N., "Zadachi sotsiologii v gradostroitel'noi nauke i proyektirovanii," *Arkhitektura SSSR,* No. 2, 1967.
Yargina, Z.N., "Nekotorye sotsial'nye aspekty perspektivnovo rasseleniya," in *Obzor arkhitekturno-sotsiologichekikh issledovaniy,* vyp. 2, Moscow, 1970.
Yeromin, I.P., "Protsess urbanizatsii v Novosibirskoi oblasti," in *Kratkoye soderzhanie dokladov XXVII nauchno-tekhnicheskoi konferentsii. Sektsiya arkhitektury,* Novosibirsk, 1970.
Zhuchenko, V.S., Steshenko, V.S. (eds.), *Vliyanie sotsial'no-ekonomicheskikh faktorov na demograficheskie protsessy,* Kiev, 1972.

Section 2. On Foreign Countries

Baranov, A.V., "Issledovanie urbanizatsii v amerikanskoi sotsiologii," *Voprosy filosofii,* No. 2, 1971.
Bonifatyeva, L.I., "K voprosu ob urbanizatsii Tseilona," *Voprosy geografii,* No. 64, 1964.
Bonifatyeva, L.I., "K voprosu ob opredelenii urovnya urbanizatsii Indii," in *Strany i narody Vostoka,* vyp. V, Moscow, 1967.
Bonifatyeva, L.I., "Nekotorye osobennosti urbanizatsii Yuzhnoi i Yugo-Vostochnoi Azii," in *Materialy Vtorovo mezhduvedomstvennovo soveshchaniya po geografii naseleniya,* vyp. 2, Moscow, 1968.
Braginsky, M.I., "Urbanizatsiya i afrikansky proletariat," in *Urbanizatsiya i rabochiy klass v usloviakh nauchno-tekhnicheskoi revolyutsii,* Moscow, 1970.
Dolinin, A.A., "Osobennosti urbanizatsii v Latinskoi Amerike," *zvestiya Vsesoyuznovo geograficheskovo obshchestva,* No. 6, 1971.
Donde, A.S., "Osobennosti protsessov urbanizatsii v razvivayushchikhsya stranakh (na primere Zapadnoi Afriki)," in *Doklady komissii geografii naseleniya i gorodov,* vyp. 2(4), Leningrad, 1965.
Gavrilova, A.F., "Svoyeobrazie protsessov urbanizatsii v Nigerii," *Sovetskaya etnografiya,* No. 3, 1969.

Guzevaty, Ya. N., *Problemy narodonaseleniya i sotsial'no-ekonomicheskoye razvitie stran Azii, Afriki i Latinskoi Ameriki,* Moscow, 1970. (see particularly Chap. 2 Vnutrennyaya migratsiya i urbanizatsiya).
Koval', B.I., *Problema urbanizatsii v sovremennoi Brazilii,* Moscow, 1964.
Krupyanko, M.I., "Osnovnye problemy urbanizatsii Yaponii," in Nekrasov, N.N. (ed.), *Sostoyanie i problemy razmeshcheniya proizvoditel'nykh sil Yaponii,* Moscow, 1968.
Krupyanko, M.I., "Protsessy urbanizatsii v osveshchenii yaponskikh geografov," *Izvestiya AN SSSR.* Seriya geograficheskaya, No. 5, 1971.
Lappo, G.M., "Urbanizatsiya v kapitalisticheskikh stranakh Zapadnoi Yevropy," *Voprosy geografii,* No. 66, Moscow, 1965.
Lipets, Yu. G., *Sovremennye migratsionnye protsessy i urbanizatsiya v Yuzhnoi i Severnoi Rodezii,* Moscow, 1964.
Mashbits, Ya. G., "Latinskaya Amerika: urbanizatsiya i sotsial'no-ekonomicheskoye razvitie," *Mirovaya ekonomika i mezhdunarodnye otnosheniya,* No. 10, 1966.
Mashbits, Ya. G., "Masshtaby i kharakter urbanizatsii v Latinskoi Amerike," in *Problemy narodonaseleniya i sotsial'no-ekonomicheskoye razvitie stran Latinskoi Ameriki,* Moscow, 1971.
Mashbits. Ya. G., *Nekotorye osobennosti urbanizatsii v Latinskoi Amerike,* Moscow, 1964.
Maslov, V.A., Shakhnovich, K.A., "Nekotorye osobennosti urbanizatsii b stranakh Vostochnoi Afriki," *Voprosy geogrefii naseleniya i naselyonnykh punktov,* Leningrad, 1970.
Mikhailov, Ye. D., "Nekotorye sotsial'nye aspekty krizisa gorodov," *SShA,* No. 7, 1971.
Nitoburg, E.L., "Suburbanizatsiya i negrityanskie getto v SShA," *Sovetskaya etnografiya,* No. 5, 1968.
Oganova, A.S., "Nekotorye problemy izucheniya protsessa urbanizatsii v razvivayushchikhsya stranakh Azii, Afriki i Latinskoi Ameriki," in *Urbanizatsiya i rabochiy klass v usloviakh nauchno-tekhnicheskoi revolyutsii,* Moscow, 1970.
Pchelintsev, O.S., *Ekonomicheskoye obosnovanie razmeshcheniya proizvodstva. Metody, primenyayemye v kapitalisticheskikh stranakh,* Moscow, 1966.
Pchelintsev, O.S., "Ekonomicheskie posledstviya sovremennovo razvitiya kapitalistichekikh gorodov (po materialam burzhuaznoi pechati)," *Voprosy ekonomiki,* No. 1, 1967.
Pimenova, R.A., "Nekotorye osobennosti urbanizatsii Argentiny," *Latinskaya Amerika,* No. 5, 1970.
Pivovarov, Yu. L., "Urbanizatsiya v sotsialisticheskikh stranakh zarubezhnoi Yevropy," *Izvestiya AN SSSR.* eriya geograficheskaya, No. 5, 1966.
Pivovarov, Yu. L., "Urbanizatsiya i rost gorodskovo naseleniya mira v XX veke," *Izvestiya AN SSSR.* Seriya geograficheskaya, No. 5, 1970.
Pokatayeva, T., "Urbanizatsiya v razvivayushchikhsya stranakh," *Mirovaya ekonomika i mezhdunarodnye otnosheniya,* No. 9, 1969.

Pokshishevsky, V.V., *Geografiya naseleniya zarubezhnykh stran,* Moscow, 1971 (see section on Goroda i protsessy urbanizatsii).
Pokshishevsky, V.V., *Ob izuchenii urbanizatsii razvivayushchikhsya stran i svyazannykh s neyu etnicheskikh protsessov,* Moscow, 1964.
Pokshishevsky, V.V., Gokhman, V.M., "Problemy giperurbanizatsii v razvitykh kapitalisticheskikh stranakh i yeyo geograficheskie aspekty," in *Nauchnye problemy geografii naseleniya,* Moscow Univ., 1967.
Ponomarchuk, O.I., "Urbanizatsiya prichiny i sledstviya," in *Latinskaya Amerike: demograficheskiy vzryv,* Moscow, 1971.
Pulyakin, V.A., *Protsess urbanizatsii v Afganistane,* Moscow, 1964.
Rakovsky, S.N., "Urbanizatsiya v zarubszhnysk sotsialisticheskikh stranakh Yevropy," *Geografiya v shkole,* No. 2, 1969.
Shiryayev, B.A., "V stikhii urbanizatsii. Besplodnye popytki regulirovaniya sotsial'nykh protsessov v amerikanskikh gorodakh," *Stroitel'stvo i arkhitektura Leningrada,* No. 11, 1970.
Urlanis, B. Ts., *Dinamika i struktura naseleniya SSSR i SShA,* Moscow, 1964.
Utkin, G.N., "Urbanizatsiya i formirovanie promyshlenosti v severo-afrikanskikh gorodakh," in *Geografiya i razvivayushchiyesya strany (Problemy ispol'zovaniya prirodnykh i trudovykh resursov). Tezisy dokladov,* Moscow, 1970.
Yanitsky, O.N., "Urbanizirovannaya Amerika: sotsiologicheskie problemy goroda budushchevo," *Mirovaya ekonomika i mezhdunarodnye otnosheniya,*

No. 8, 1969.
Yanitsky, O.N., "Urbanizatsiya i kapitalisticheskoye obshchestvo," *Mirovaya ekonomika i mezhdunarodnye otnosheniya,* No. 7, 1971.
Yargina, Z.N., "Napravlennost' i problematika zapadnoi sotsiologii goroda," in *Arkhitekturno-sotsiologicheskie issledovaniya (Obzor),* vyp. 1, Moscow, 1970.
Zinovieva, R.A., "Urbanizatsiya i izmenenie sotsial'noi struktury v Latinskoi Amerike," in *Urbanizatsiya i rabochiy klass v usloviakh nauchno-tekhnicheskoi revolyutsii,* Moscow, 1970.

LIBRARY OF DAVIDSON COLLEGE

on regular loan may be checked out for two
sented at the Circulation Desk in or

rged after date due.

re subject to special regulatio.